38 Pieces of Shrapnel

Copyright © 2014 Fred Oerly.
First Edition, July 2014

Printed in the United States of America
ISBN: 9 781616 004613

Editor: Meredith Ludwig
Designer: Ginny Booker

Printed by Mizzou Publishing book services at The Mizzou Store

38 PIECES OF SHRAPNEL

FRED OERLY

Edited by Meredith Ludwig

Fred Oerly, participant in a 2010 Honor Flight to Washington, D.C.

You can purchase a copy of this book signed by Fred, AND help the **Central Missouri Honor Flight** give our veterans the respect and appreciation they deserve! The book sells for $15 and the Central Missouri Honor Flight retains the proceeds above the book's cost of production.

For information on Central Missouri Honor Flight, visit the organization's web site: **centralmissourihonorflight.com**.

My appreciation

First and foremost, I wish to thank my Lieutenant Charles B. Pearson of Frisco Texas, and assure him the first copy of this book is his as requested.

Creating a book and permanent digital archive of my stories of World War II takes a lot of work, and there are many who deserve my appreciation, including:

- My editor, Meredith Ludwig, who went the extra mile to bring both my books to fruition.

- The designer, Ginny Booker, whose labor of love made both my books attractive and effective.

- John Mier, who spent many hours typing my notebooks full of hand-written notes and for helping the book take shape.

- My daughter Donavan Davis, my niece Carol Warren, and John Hopkins, who helped improve and refine the content.

- My grandson, Mitchell Hughey, who conducted my interview for the Library of Congress, Veterans History Project, and who read the book aloud and assembled and edited the audio files so those who cannot read it can listen to it.

- My doctors, Wade Schondelmeyer and Eric Thompson, and all the health care workers who kept me alive long enough for this dream to become a reality.

- The University of Missouri's MOspace for keeping a digital archive of this book, along with the preparatory materials and the audio files; and Heather Tearney of Mizzou Publications at the Mizzou Store where both my books were printed.

- And especially my daughter, Diane Oerly, for persistence above and beyond the call of duty to help me share my stories and enjoy my life.

Finally if you know someone who is losing their sight, like me, PLEASE NOTE: a spoken copy of this book and other digital materials are available online. Just visit: mospace.umsystem.edu and search for "Fred Oerly."

Sincerely,

Fred Oerly

Age 91, July 2014

38 Pieces of Shrapnel
Memories of World War II in the Pacific
by Fred Oerly

TIMELINE
of Oscar Fred Oerly's Military Service in the Pacific

December 7, 1941	Japanese bomb Pearl Harbor on Fred's 19th birthday.
September 5, 1942	(Oscar) Fred Oerly enlisted in US Marines in Kansas City, MO. - Following Boot Camp in San Diego, Fred attended twelve weeks of training in Los Angeles, CA.
Mid January, 1943	Boarded ship for thirty-eight day trip to New Caledonia (7,726 miles from home).
Late February, 1943	Fred arrives in New Caledonia and spends some three months wiring the island – they strung 20 pair telephone cable from one end of the island to the other.
Late June, 1943	Fred's first stay on Guadalcanal lasts approximately four months.
October, 1943	Fred makes his first amphibious landing (in Higgins boats) on Bougainville. He fought for approximately three weeks. When the fighting was over, he had blood poisoning (poisoned bamboo pit) and was flown to hospital on Guadalcanal.
Nov. – Dec., 1943	Fred spends approximately two months in hospital recovering.
Spring, 1944	Fred catches up with his brother on Guadalcanal, and serves under Sam briefly.
July, 1944	Fred and Sam make a landing together on Guam as part of the 3rd Division. Fred spends more than six months on Guam – a prolonged stay because there were US civilians on the island to protect.
December, 1944	Fred returns to Guadalcanal – at this point the Sixth division of the Marines was created and Fred became a part of the Sixth JASU (Joint Assault Signal Corps.)

April 1, 1945	Landing on Okinawa (Easter Sunday). Navy frogmen and the naval observers go onto the island first for reconnaissance. Fought for several weeks and made their way from the north to south side of Okinawa where they were put aboard ship for an amphibious landing on the southern shore.
May 8, 1945	V-E Day (Victory in Europe Day), marks Nazi Germany's unconditional surrender and the end of World War II in Europe.
August 6 & 9, 1945	Atomic bombs dropped on Hiroshima and Nagasaki Japan. Having suffered injuries on Okinawa, Fred is hospitalized at the time.
September 2, 1945	Surrender of Japan occurred aboard the battleship USS Missouri in Tokyo Bay. Lt. Pearson and rest of the unit are aboard ship in the bay prepared for a double-cross.
November, 1945	Fred returns home with 38 pieces of shrapnel in his body. Discharged November 13, 1945. Fred and Jan are engaged on Thanksgiving and married on Christmas, 1945.

Places Served

The trip aboard ship from San Diego, CA to the South Pacific took 38 days. To avoid enemy submarine attack, they zigzagged across the ocean and crossed the equator six times. With Guadalcanal as a base camp, Fred traveled to:

New Caledonia
Guadalcanal
Bougainville
Guadalcanal
Guam
Guadalcanal
Saipan & Tinian
Guadalcanal
Okinawa
Guadalcanal

Injuries and Honors

Fred was significantly injured several times during his 38 months as a Marine including:

1.   Bougainville – stepped into poison bamboo pit. Spent approximately two months in hospital.

2.   Guadalcanal – while stretching wire for telephone service, the pole broke. Spent 3 days in hospital.

3.   Okinawa – inside the caves his friend next to him tripped a land mine and was killed. Spent eight days in amputee ward on hospital ship, then several months recovering. Was in hospital when they dropped the atomic bombs on Japan.

4.   Guadalcanal – at war's end, while loading the ship and awaiting orders to go in and occupy Japan, a load of rock fell on his left hand and crushed it. He was unable to go with this unit to occupy Japan, and was sent back to the states and discharged on November 13, 1945.

Fred was awarded a Purple Heart, a Bronze Star, and a Presidential Citation.

Source:

http://www.benning.army.mil/library/content/Virtual/Donovanpapers/maps/
StudentMaps/BanksDavid/MapA.jpg

Source:

http://www.benning.army.mil/library/content/Virtual/Donovanpapers/maps/StudentMaps/BanksDavid/MapB.jpg

BEARS

There are many books written about the war, but I realize only someone who has been there can convey a true understanding. If you find somebody who is willing to share that part of his or her life, it's a good idea to settle in and listen. I do not sit around pondering all the bad memories from the war. I have a great hobby as a wood carver and spend much time whittling, carving and painting things out of wood. Many days pass when I do not even think about being a Marine. But there are still times, after over 70 years, when I have dreams that are not pleasant, dreams that some would describe as nightmares.

I want to dedicate this book to Vern Hartmann, a veteran who lived at Hartmann Village, a senior living center in my hometown of Boonville, Missouri. I'll begin with a letter to him.

Dear Vern,

I know you are wondering what those ruggedly carved bears were doing on your table where you eat lunch. I can hear you saying, "What the hell is this?!" I'll try to explain.

When I was serving a tour of duty on Okinawa, I met a young Marine who was sent there to replace a fellow who had lost his life defending his country. Since he was replacing someone special, he won a place in my heart and we very rapidly became good friends.

I know you are responsible for sending a young reporter to my home and when Edward came for the interview. I was working on a large sack of bears determined to get them finished and put away. I should never have tried to carve twenty-two of these ugly bears at one time. It might have been why I was having so many bad dreams as I whittled on them before retiring to bed. Edward seemed to sense my drive to get them completed, but continued his interview.

One of his first questions was, "What is your birth date?" And when I answered December 7, 1922, his expression changed and he said, "How does that make you feel when Pearl Harbor Day rolls around?" I quickly answered, "Well, I haven't forgotten any of my birthdays since!"

This started me on a train of thought, and we were soon in a conversation about our country and we both expressed our wishes for many situations to change.

As the interview continued we talked about the four landings I made in my three years of service in the South Pacific. My thoughts jumped to my comrades, Private Hagen and Corporal Willy McCray.

A spotter for Air Ground Liaison, I could hear McCray's voice as he told the pilots what kind of a job they were doing. When they flew too low, strafing the enemy, he would often yell, "Pull out! Pull out!" with fear in his voice as he knew the bullets from their machine guns were going to ricochet off the earth and put an end to the life of someone we were serving with.

Private Hagen, who was then a big part of my forward observer team, was a young man of Swedish descent. He had so much blond hair he looked even taller than he was. Perhaps the reason I liked him so much was because he was always saying "Yes sir, when this crap is all over, I am going home and go bear hunting and have a bear rug made out of the first grizzly I kill and send it to you!"

This was the start of many a conversation between the two of us, each telling about our lives back home. I truly believed him when he told me that his sister was the most beautiful girl in the state of Wisconsin.

But I often wondered what the hell he thought I would do with a great big grizzly bear rug in our little four-room house. Maybe he thought it would work on our front porch where my family spent so much of our time and shared so much of our lives. We would often be vying to occupy the old handmade hickory rocking chair purchased by my dad from a friend of his. It was a crude thing but my brother never failed to remark, "The rockers on this old hand-hewn chair are as smooth as a baby's ass."

On Okinawa, a terrible night would be one where you would live through not one, not two, but three Banzai attacks. While a night may seem to be so terribly long, light in the darkness could some- times give a person a comforting feeling. I often knew this feeling because I was able to get on the radio and call for flares that could take away the darkness; suddenly the night was as bright as if the sun was shining. I was enjoying such a feeling of comfort when I saw Private Hagen standing as tall as he could and screaming aloud and stomping with all his might. My heart almost popped out of my body when I realized that I had just asked a battleship to fire three flares that would be exploding any second. I shouted at the top of my voice, "Get down, Hagen! Get down!" for those three flares would light up the night and he would surely be killed.

His answer was, "I'll get down as soon as I know this S.O.B. is dead. The only reason I am alive is because I turned to face the other way in my fox hole thinking they might attack from the other direction, and he stabbed the ground with all his might just between my knees. He was so close to me that all that crap they taught me in combat school — you know, 'Long thrust ... withdrawal ... short thrust ... withdrawal ... short jab. Nothing would work! So I simply had to jump up and stomp his brains out with the heels of my raider boots."

I said nothing back to him because I could see that he had already done what he had to do. Later I thought how I wished this experience would have ended right there, but fate would not allow it.

When the sun came up, I walked toward Hagen and said, "Hi, Hagen. How are you doing?" When he looked at me he said, "Good morning" with his usual smile, but this morning he was looking straight at me and right through me. What he was seeing were years that were gone forever, years we would never be able to get back. I had heard about combat fatigue and was now witnessing what it could do to a person. I wanted so much to say, "You know, Hagen, your sister is the prettiest girl in the state of Wisconsin." But I knew he could never hear me, and I wondered if I would ever be able to convey that message to him again.

It was now time to make a report to my lieutenant. He was only a short walk away, operating a radio, but a short walk gives a person enough time to remember how long you have known someone and how they have touched your life. On my way to talk to Lt. Pearson, I was walking past Willy McCray and when I asked him how he was doing I received no answer. When he turned his head, what I saw made my eyes fill with tears until they began to drop off my chin. There was no one-sided grin, but rather a full-faced smile, something I had never seen in the two years we had been serving together. It was difficult to see through the tears, and as I stumbled along, I knew I would have to tell my lieutenant to have the corpsman take Willy with him when he took Hagen to sick bay. You might hope memories of this night would be forgotten in a matter of days, but one's wishes and desires are often unfulfilled no matter how much prayer a person may put into them.

I never heard from Private Hagen or Corporal McCray again, but I know we all fought in the war we were told was, "the war to end all wars."

When Edward, the newspaper reporter, asked me how it made me feel to know they remember Pearl Harbor on my birthday, tears came creeping into my eyes. I wanted to say, "I have read the history of the Sixth Marine Division many times, but unless you were there, you can't really answer how it makes you feel."

When Edward left I went back to carving bears. Three of those bears are on your table to say thank you for sending Edward. He came to sit and listen and he got me thinking and writing something that feels like a book.

Your friend,

Fred and Vern

HOW IT BEGAN

My full name is Oscar Fred Oerly and I was born in Overton, Missouri, a tiny river town. As I mentioned the day was December 7 of 1922. On the very day I turned 19 years old I was living in Kansas City training to be an airplane mechanic. A friend wanted to help me celebrate my birthday so he decided to take me rabbit hunting over in Kansas. I remember we went across the bridge past the bomber plant and I told him, "That's where I'm going to be working someday."

We went to his friend's house and I asked him about the gun I was to borrow. It turned out all he had to shoot rabbits with was a 10-gauge shotgun, which is a big goose gun with a double-ought buckshot. I couldn't imagine how this was going to work, but I found a new way to hunt that day. I could let that rabbit get half way across the field and then bear down on him and take him. I thought, "Boy, this is something else." I was having me some fun, and besides, there was a nice looking girl helping scare up rabbits and I thought I should show off for her. So I shot and I shot and I shot that gun, and when I got done shooting my shoulder was black and blue.

On the way home, when we got into Kansas City, I rolled the car window down to see what the news boys were yelling about on every corner. What I heard was, "Extra! Extra! Japanese attack Pearl Harbor."

That's the first thing that I remember about the war. I hadn't been reading too much. Of course I was up on the war in Europe, but we weren't at war with Japan. It was news to me and I did not expect it. Very soon after, I was working at that bomber plant. I got me a good job making B-25s for the war. After I worked about a month I became lead man and hung the nacelles on the B-25s that came out of Kansas City. This was good experience and I was helping the war situation. I had been eager to go to work and glad to have the job, but I wasn't satisfied. I wanted to catch up with my older brother, Sam, and to do that I needed to join the Marine Corps. He'd already been in since March, 1941.

Sam was two years and two months older than me and we had a cousin, Jack, who had joined up and was a sea-going Marine aboard ship. Jack would write these letters to Sam and tell him about how great life was in the Marines and how he could enjoy himself and still save some money. At the time Sam joined there wasn't a lot of money to be made. In fact, I can remember when my brother would get up at four o'clock in the morning and go out to cut and shock corn, and if you worked really hard from sun up to sun down you could make as much as a dollar a day. When he got his chance, he grabbed it and joined the Marines.

CRABS, TRAINS AND THE ROYAL GORGE

I enlisted September 5, 1942. When I got to Kansas City, we were sworn in. One of the men also joining was the son of a Kansas lawyer and we were having some beers in the hotel where we were staying. At one point this young man's urgency to relieve himself caused him to disregard the sign in the restroom: "It does no good to stand on the seat, these Kansas City crabs can jump three feet!" Having lived in the city for a year working at the B-25 bomber plant, when I read the sign, I went to my room to go to the toilet. This lawyer's son got the crabs and our platoon had to stay put until we all had a clean bill of health. My first three days in the Marines were served under the order, "Confined to Quarters!"

The next big move, as I started my tour of duty, was to march in formation from our hotel to Union Station. What a pleasure it would have been, standing on the curb and watching these boots march by. I am sure it was more enjoyable than watching "Gomer Pyle," but I often thought he might have gotten some ideas for his show from the way we marched on our first attempt.

Our trip to LA aboard the troop train was a rather pleasant experience. There was a dining car and the food was very good. A great number of men had joined the service, and we seemed to be appreciated by the people we met along the way. We got to stop at a number of locations to view the wonders of our western states. On the trip I bought a metal trinket for my mom. It was a scene of the Royal Gorge and I mailed it to her. After my tour of duty was up and I got to go home, I would see it tied to a long string on the light in our living room. It had hung there all the time I had been away.

DAY ONE

The first day of basic training is one a Marine never forgets. The uniform of the day was not buckskin but rather buck naked! Walking around barefooted did not seem to be significant to me because I never wore shoes from the time school was out in the spring until it resumed in the fall. I had trained my eyes to see things that shouldn't be stepped on, or would cut or bruise my feet. One of the men in my group stepped on a big gob of chewing gum and squashed it between his toes. I never should have laughed at him, for I found it much harder to convince him that we should be friends.

As you march around in your all-together, you learn that your next major task will be to get basic shots. That means a shot for every disease known to exist in the boundaries of the United States and all the islands in the South Pacific.

We then entered one of the large buildings surrounding the parade field. Once inside we saw three lines forming. They were headed to the other side of the building with a small sign over the door that simply says, "Exit." At this point you have a bucket hanging on your elbow which is carrying a lone toothbrush. You begin to wonder why you have been given a bucket to carry around all day and you have nothing to put in it except your toothbrush. You could put the toothbrush in your pocket and get along fine. No! Wait a minute! This is a special day and you have no pockets!

There is a doctor standing on each side of the line. Each doctor has two assistants with a needle in each hand, filled to capacity, ready for action. Each doctor has a smile on his face as his duty of the day begins. Now you will learn why there has been nothing but a toothbrush placed in each bucket. As the doctors stick the needle home, there will be heard either an "Ouch!" "Ow!" "Damn!" or some other remark. Each outburst will be followed by what we later referred to as "the toothbrush boogie," a dance the soldiers did as they shook off the pain of the shots, the toothbrush clanging all the while in their buckets. This should have been enough fun for the first day of any organization, but there was still a great deal of sunlight in the days during the month of September.

Next was a march to the barber shop where our load would be lightened. The line stopped at the door and each time the buzz from the clippers would stop, the barricade was lowered and another person stepped inside. Without being there, you can't imagine how many different shaped heads showed up after they'd been run over by a set of clippers. There were thin elongated shapes, flat ones, out of round and some come to a sharp peak. Some are square and blocky or curved the wrong way, like they were left lying in an odd position too long. For every description imaginable there was a hair cut to fit it. When you saw yourself for the first time in the mirror, you didn't know whether to burst out laughing or sit down and have a good cry.

The bucket was not issued to you because Marines go around camp carrying a bucket of water, but was rather used to carry all your possessions. It was also issued for an important training session that all wartime Marines are acquainted with. At any time, you were subjected to the order of your platoon leader to dump your belongings and put your bonnet on. You were expected to stand at attention and place the bucket over your head. Then you had to start yelling, "I am a Shit Head!" in a rather loud voice. Several marching maneuvers and orders were given, and once the leader was satisfied the person wearing the metal bonnet was headed in the right direction, the instructor would give the command, "Double time. March!"

Of course you cannot see where you are going if you have a metal bucket over your head. Now you are being instructed to march twice as fast so you run into a lot of things. The crash between a plywood shack and a new recruit won't easily be forgotten. Even though I have never been given such an order, I have witnessed many of my friends take such commands. If the sound of the crash did not seem loud enough, there would be some instructor close by to deliver several thumps with his swagger stick until he felt the training was complete. The only benefit was you would never need to wear earplugs if you were lucky enough to get in an artillery unit. This type of training left several of my friends' buckets out of round, and I would often see them give their bonnets a twist or two in the sand to get it to set upright.

At this point I still didn't have a uniform, but on to the dentist I went to have three teeth filled without pain killers. But maybe my nakedness was a plus for I seemed to not feel the misery as much as if I had been fully clothed.

A loud whistle called our group into formation. For those who did not know where they belonged, the DI, drill instructor, had a swagger stick and helped them find their place. "Good job, Men!" the DI would always yell. It was time to get our uniforms. The Quartermaster building was filled with wire cages from floor to ceiling and it was obvious they had been better stocked in the past than they were this day. As we were marched past each cage, it was our duty to shout out the size we wore. It made no difference what you said because the old, beer-gutted, heavily-tattooed quartermaster reached for the next pile of clothing and threw it at you. Most of that night was spent in a uniform exchange as we tried to trade each item for one that was nearer our size.

Next I witnessed my surprise of the day. It was now time to issue us our field shoes and the same type procedure was used. You walked by, shouted out your size and hoped to get something that came close. As the group sat around trying on their shoes, there seemed to be a rumble in the room and soon it became clear, "These shoes don't fit me!"

"They will tomorrow!" was shouted back at us and we were marched to a shower room. After placing our bucket and recently-issued uniforms against the wall in a neat row, we were told to find a shower. Immediately, on came the hot water, salt water and as a reward for doing so well this day, we were given a two-hour shoe-fitting shower. We were then told if we wanted shoes that fit us and made no blisters, we would wear them all night. You may be surprised to learn the man was right. Each pair was tenderized by soaking in hot salt water and then by wearing them until dry, they formed to your feet.

THE FIRST BLACK MARINES

The warm weather of California was the reason for my choosing to go to boot camp in San Diego rather than training at Parris Island in North Carolina. But make no mistake, either place can put a chill on your body that will run up and down your spine. When the cool breeze comes in gently and begins to give you a salt water moistening, beware of conditions that may follow. Such was the evening when we were enjoying our first night in San Diego. There were many complaints about being cold, and the question was asked, "Does anyone know how to light these kerosene heaters?" Of course, there was one guy who claimed to know more about kerosene heaters than the man who invented them. He rapidly began the job of turning on the two heaters that were in our plywood shack that was called our quarters. He rolled up a piece of newspaper and put a match to it and soon had both our burners percolating. That's one of the advantages of being a member of such a large group. There is someone who knows something about any problem and is willing to offer his help.

The next morning, I was lying there contemplating the day that was ahead of us when I heard someone in a rather gruff voice ask, "Who is the smart ass who lit the kerosene burners? And why do I have a taste in my mouth like I slept under a turkey roost all night?" I looked at that man and there were just two circles where his eyes were and the rest of him was coal black. That fellow had turned those heaters up so high that the room was just filled with soot and it was all over us and our equipment. There were no black men in the Marine Corps at that time, so we were the very first. It was funny, but what a mess it was to clean up.

The first joy on my second day in the Marines was surely the fact that they let you sleep until 5:30 AM. Then we were awakened by a bugle. The Marine who was playing the bugle got that duty in the same manner as everyone did. A question would be asked like, "Is there anyone here who has a driver's license?" When he replied, "I have!" he was told, "Here, drive this wheelbarrow over to the parade grounds. You are now in charge of picking up all the cigarette butts! When you joined the Marines, you were given a choice of occupations. When you wrote down 'vehicle driver,' didn't you know wheelbarrows were included?" But it wasn't all bad because the very day I joined the Marine Corps so did the Hollywood actor Tyrone Power. I drove my wheelbarrow right along beside his, and both of us joined in the special task of keeping the parade grounds butt free.

We had twelve weeks of basic training and that should be enough for any servicemen before they boarded a troop ship for overseas duty. We had learned how to march in formation and most importantly how to distinguish your Drill Instructor's voice above all other noises. That should be your first task. Otherwise, you will be marching around with your three-gallon bucket over your head. And if your instructor believes he is a drummer, like the great Gene Krupa, he'll get into a rhythm and won't stop whacking the beat on your bonnet.

A PRESIDENTIAL VISIT

One day in basic training had been set aside for the President of the United States to visit the Marine Corps Base and the Naval Station. It had been announced for weeks before he came to see us. This base was given a complete overhaul. There was a smell of fresh paint everywhere! Even the asphalt parade grounds had been camouflaged to look as if cows had been happily grazing on the fresh grass, filling their stomachs to capacity so they could join the rest of the herd who were lying in the shade. They had literally painted the blacktop to look like a cow pasture. The cow poop had been painted by an artist and was so realistic it caused a reflex action from all us country boys who were being taught to march in formation. No boy raised on a farm could look down and see a big pile of cow manure and step right in it. He would break rank and cause such confusion that several platoons had to be held over for another week and taught the side straddle hop to keep from breaking rank.

This was a big thing for me since I had never seen a President before and I was really looking forward to it, but we had to stand at attention so long that a number of the men fainted. The officers kept dragging them behind the formations so the President couldn't see them.

The President arrived in a big, long automobile and we watched as he put a cigarette in a long holder and tapped a man's shoulder for him to light it. After only a couple of puffs, he gave it to the man and made a very nice speech. I really can't remember too much of what he said because I kept wondering who would find the cigarette butt that President Roosevelt had thrown away.

The letter I wrote my mother about his visit mentioned how excited I was and quoted him as saying,

"Men, you will soon be going overseas! Some of you will not return! I promise to each of you that the job you held when you joined will be waiting for you when you return. There will be on-the-job training if you need it and each of you will receive free medical attention for the rest of your life!"

It was a great feeling to have someone who had overcome so many hardships in his life to now be my Commander in Chief. In my letter I tried to convince my mother how lucky I had been to be only a few yards from the spot where he had chosen to give his speech. At the time I had no idea I would be in the U.S. Marines thirty-eight months and never receive a furlough.

I liked President Roosevelt. I also liked President Truman. Perhaps that was because he was from my state. Or maybe it was simply because he was our last president to answer a question with a single "Yes!" or "No!" never trying to answer a question with another question.

SUBMARINE ATTACK

At one point in basic training I was daydreaming and counting my blessings as a boot Marine when I was startled back to reality by the shrill sound of the air-raid sirens on the base. They were joined by all the sirens at the Naval Station as well as the ones on all the ships in the harbor. The scuttlebutt spread like wild fire. "Submarines sighted just outside our harbor! Air raid! It's an air raid!"

All the planes in the vicinity were trying to become airborne. Any floating object that was able to maneuver was immediately sent out to sea. The destroyers began to shoot off depth charges and the battleships maneuvered into position.

Even 12 dirigibles were sent high into the sky. The cables that tethered them stopped any planes from attacking our base in a strafing formation. Of course, the balloons also did a super job of accurately spotting the exact size and location of our Marine Corps base and seemed to me to be a great help to the enemy. This made the thousands of dollars spent camouflaging our base wasted and the piles of cow manure painted in the pastures useless.

After the depth charges were fired all the uproar shut down pretty quick. The excitement was almost too much even for this old country boy. There were articles in the paper for many days after this great scare telling each Marine, Sailor, Seabee and Army personnel how glad the public was that we were in the area and how much safer they felt with us there.

CASUALTIES COME TOO SOON

Death seemed to find us as soon as training started. It did not wait for us to get overseas. My platoon had its first casualty in boot camp. We were on a training session to learn how to jump into a swimming pool wearing a full pack, helmet, weapon or other special equipment we might need. If you survived the jump, then your duty was to swim around or stay afloat for a two-hour period. We were divided into the buddy system and wound up with one extra. A volunteer said, "I won't need a buddy. I was a lifeguard for two years in a swimming pool in Los Angeles."

After the training session was over, the whistle was blown to clear the pool and that lifeguard was found on the bottom. They were unable to revive him and it was such a sad day. I was a ScoutMaster for 12 years after I was discharged and used the buddy system all those years, but if we ever came up with an extra, there were three men that each had two buddies to watch out for. I often thought of this young man and give him the credit for an accident-free time in scouting.

Jacques Farm was a tank training encampment, and was the site of another training casualty. One of our men went to a clump of brush to rest for a few moments in the shade. A tank driver saw the brush, and not knowing anyone was behind it thought he would show off a bit and make a good impression. He ran his tank over the brush and flattened it with just a few twists and turns. When he finished he zipped that tank around and sped back in formation. Our man was unable to get out of his way in time and lost his life that day because of some meaningless antics.

During a drill in the middle of the night the order went out to pack our seabags, head to the beach and right out into the ocean. One man didn't make it back. It was total foolishness. No one should be rushed out to sea from a deep sleep like that.

Another time, we were learning to crawl on our bellies, and they were shooting live rounds of ammunition over our heads to impress upon us the importance of staying down. This one fellow crawled up on a rattlesnake and of course he jumped up.

These men died before they ever went to war. The careless ways in which we lost them, makes their deaths all the harder to bear.

EXPERT MARKSMAN

Camp Matthews was where all Marines who were based in San Diego were sent to be trained in the use of weapons. This was where you learned how to fire pistols and rifles, how to protect yourself with the bayonet, and how to inflict hurt on the enemy. Over and over and over again we would practice until our instructors were satisfied with our actions. There was a lot of grumbling and bitching, but I am satisfied that many feel the same as I do when I say, "Thank you for all the training I received."

When it came to shooting a rifle I had a homegrown advantage. My mother gave me a pump-up air rifle for my eighth birthday. She had bought it through our grocery store when it was on sale during the summer. The bottom of the cedar chest seemed a good place to hide it until time for Christmas. My little sister, Hazel, found it and told me where it was. She thought it was for my older brother Sam and it would be all right to tell me.

After finding where it was, I had to check on it each day, and soon thought it wouldn't hurt to take it down the railroad track and try it out one time. That one time turned into many times and when I received it for my Christmas present, my mother sure embarrassed me by writing all over the stock of the gun, "Damaged in shipment. These spots do not interfere with reliability of weapon. Do not repair. Use as is." My mother was a very wise person. A good spanking would have been much easier but less effective.

I got my first .22 rifle for Christmas just after my ninth birthday, along with access to free ammunition. Anytime I wanted a box of cartridges, I was allowed to go to dad's store and get a free box. I learned to shoot a rifle by shooting a rifle.

We went up to Camp Matthews for a whole week. I really tried hard to do well, and it was my goal to be expert rifleman, expert pistol and expert bayonet. When I wrote my brother and told him what I wanted to do, he wrote back and suggested I try for only one, saying expert rifle is the most important and is probably the one they pay most attention to when they consider a Marine for advancement.

A rather unusual experience happened while I was firing my weapon at camp for record. I was so disappointed on the day we fired, because as I fired from the prone position I became very sick to my stomach and stopped for a few minutes to see if I could get to feeling better. I remembered laying there hoping I might get over it and able to start again when a jeep pulled up about 20 feet in front of the firing line and stopped. Then the driver drove it back to its original place. Since I was a Corporal, I thought it was only right to give him a warning, so when he started to drive by again, I stood up to yell at him. "Hey boot! They put dumbbells in the brig for the trick you are pulling!" Come to find out there was no one in that jeep. The next thing I heard was, "Earthquake! Cease fire! Earthquake!" I was so relieved to find out that my upset stomach was from the quaking of the earth and not from the smell of gunpowder or I could never have reached my goal.

Qualification day was and always will be a day of excitement. My father had spent a great deal of time telling me how important records were in controlling your base pay. He stressed how much easier it was to be advanced to the next rank if a good record was going ahead of you. So it was a great pleasure for me to write my father a letter telling him that I could now dress in a Marine Corps uniform and legally wear the medals Expert Rifle, Expert Bayonet and Expert Pistol. And it was a further pleasure for me to tell him that I had made the highest score of anyone qualifying on the rifle range that day.

Only two out of a large number of Marines had shot expert rifle that day and we had a great surprise. We were invited to the colonel's quarters after our shower and were greeted with a highball in each hand. This was breaking a great number of rules and regulations, but I was sure glad to be a part of this celebration.

To make a good day even better, the colonel offered each of us a job as trainer on his rifle range, and a guarantee that we would become permanent personnel on his team for the duration of the war. An offer so fantastic was a hard thing to believe, but I had already been offered permanent labor at the B-25 airplane plant in Kansas City before I joined the Marines. The decision was very hard to make. My plan had always been to transfer to any unit my brother was serving in. I also wondered if I was really that good a shot. The reason I did so well was because my father taught me about Kentucky windage, an adjustment a shooter makes for the wind or the motion of the target. 90 percent of the Marines shooting that day would have never heard of such a thing. I asked the other Marine, "What state are you from?" His answer was "Kentucky"!

The flavor of the highball helped me put things in their proper perspective, and I gave my reasons for not accepting the offer, even though I felt that the colonel would surely be a good person to work for. Never again was such an offer sent in my direction, but I still remember the pleasure I had when shooting my rapid-fire session and seeing the result signal raised and spun in a fashion that I had never seen before. I knew I was having a good day.

THE BEST I'VE EVER KNOWN

The two corporals assigned the duty of taking my platoon through training were and still are the best I have ever known. Both men had been in the Marines a number of years and served overseas, and neither one had a tattoo. As I let my mind wander back through the years to the short time that I shared a portion of my life with these two corporals, I am amazed that I can still remember their names.

Cpl. Krohn gave me great advice when it came to finding a comrade. He told me to choose one fellow, go on liberty with him, and get skunk drunk. Pay particular attention to his actions, let him lead the conversation all night until you are sure of his likes and dislikes, and make your decision based on his behavior. If you choose him to be your partner, will he stand guard while you sleep? Will he have a caring attitude about you? Are you sure he is the one you can put your trust in? The way he acts when he is inebriated is the way he'll feel about you when the chips are down and your life may well depend upon his good decisions.

Everyone liked Cpl. Benson. He was the one who chose me to be leader of my squad, which was an automatic advancement to the next rank. This made me feel great to make P.F.C. (Private First Class) so rapidly, and I could hardly wait to write my brother who had been in service long enough to be a Master Sergeant.

Even though he seemed to be several years our senior, Cpl. Benson was in touch with everyone and knew their likes and dislikes. As I was doing my laundry with my scrub brush and my cake of P & G soap (Proctor & Gamble) he strolled by and said hello to everyone doing laundry. The shout of laundry inspection gave me no reason to worry because I was completely through with that chore. So I nonchalantly fell into formation.

As the corporal continued his inspection, he took a step sideways and looked me up and down. I was standing at attention as I should have been. With a quick jerk I felt the pair of green shorts I was holding out for inspection leave my hand and fall to the sand in front of my feet. Two or three stomps with his left foot was enough to make me understand that I was not through laundering my clothes, and as he took a step sideways his left foot gathered enough sand to make it look like a miniature bulldozer had deposited every grain of it right on top of my underwear. "Report to my tent after inspection" was the order that I could hardly believe.

After inspection was over, I went straight to his tent and tapped gently on his door before saying, "P.F.C. Oerly reporting as requested, Sir!" I heard "Come in" answered as if nothing had happened. Upon entering I was told to have a seat. I sat down slowly, feeling that maybe I had a hearing problem or at least had become very confused. Cpl. Benson said, "I know you need an explanation of my actions at inspection, so I invited you here to explain." Before I could control myself, I blurted out, "But Corporal, those were the cleanest shorts on this base!" He said, "The action I took today may someday save your life. It is very necessary that you have the respect of each person under your control, and what I did today makes each one of the men respect you. You are now one of them, and if any man ever gets his laundry stomped in the sand — which they will — you will hear them say, 'P.F.C. Oerly was the first to get a crotch of San Diego sand.' It was that or the bucket bonnet, and I hope you preferred what happened today." I never received a smile from Cpl. Benson without feeling that he understood me.

I want to convey one more thing about Cpl. Benson that took place during basic training. It was probably the time my body was filled with fear more than any other time in training. I sensed a rift in my squad between two boys who came from different backgrounds and were of different nationalities, but I never knew there was such a difficult feeling between them. It was almost like they were getting a letter from their grandmother every day telling them to whip up on the other one. I came into our barracks to find these two squared off and jumping around like fighting cocks. I knew I was in a great deal of trouble when I saw they both had switchblades. If it had been possible to do so, I would have turned time back to the day I arrived on the base and would gladly have given my advancement back to Cpl. Benson. My sudden urge to yell for him right then was hard to control.

When I was growing up there was a man that came to our grocery store that had a terrible scar, and I knew him well enough to ask him how he got such a scar. He informed me that he had been in a knife fight, and he told me the only way to win one of those fights is to avoid it. With that in mind I walked between those two men and kept on walking until I got to my bunk. I sat down and grabbed my rifle and put my bayonet on it. Then I said very slowly, trying to keep my voice from shaking, "Go ahead and have your big fight, but remember, the one who wins has to fight me next and I don't have a knife so I'll have to use my rifle with the bayonet fixed." Both boys agreed they really didn't want to fight. I often look back and wondered if one little stripe on your shirt sleeve meant anything, or maybe Cpl. Benson was right — they now felt that I was one of them.

FREE TIME AND SCHOOLING

Every chance I got I would go to the San Diego Zoo. I used to go to Swope Park Zoo when I was living in Kansas City, but this one was even bigger and better. But, of course I did more than just go to the zoo.

I got liberty one time and I remember we went to a big bar. It was packed with so many Navy and Marine Corps personnel and the place was just too small so a fist fight broke out. Lehmeyer, the boy I was with, said "Follow me," and he got down on his hands and knees, got under the table and we crawled our way out of that bar and out onto the street. Then he said, "Stand up and walk natural." I did exactly that. I stood up and walked behind him, and we eased on past all the MPs who had come there to arrest the servicemen and throw them in the paddy wagon. When we got to the corner we ran as fast as we could to get out of there.

I had not gotten to go to college, but the Marine Corps offered all kinds of correspondence courses so this was my chance. I enjoyed writing to tell them what classes I wanted and I signed up for several, including trigonometry and other math courses. It really was just like going to college. I could sit there at night, write letters to these people and take my tests.

I received the highest grade of anyone in the platoon, and at the end of basic training got to go to Telephone School in Los Angeles for 12 weeks. My older sister, Marie, was living nearby. I could get on a streetcar, run to her house and take a visit.

I remember being very proud of the unit I was in when stationed in Los Angeles. We would march down the streets from our quarters to a building owned by the Bell Telephone Company, which had volunteered to train servicemen placed in the field of communications. We were a classy group, and pretty young girls would run along beside us and talk to us as we marched. The girls' families would stand and cheer as we passed them and it seemed great to be a Marine. Those 12 weeks are possibly the best memories I have of the tour of duty I served.

Our unit was housed in a Japanese school building that had been taken over by the US Government. It had been abandoned when the Japanese were moved to interment camps. Most of the Japanese people living in the Los Angeles area were simply gathered up and transported to what we called a "campsite" and they had to abandon all their buildings. If they could prove they were Americans they could join the Marine Corps.

It wasn't a pleasant thing for me to think about because I thought it was unfair, breaking up families, confiscating their property, telling them they would take care of it and see that they got it back. But I don't think it always worked that way and I didn't feel it was right. I think later on there were a lot of people in America who felt the same as I did. It lasted for a long, long time and it seemed like many were very, very slow in being released. After I was discharged from the Marine Corps I was working in LA, and for about two years after the war ended, there were still people in camps. Not only did they have to release them, but they had to give back their land and their buildings. It took time and it was quite confusing for Americans who were using the property and most certainly for the Japanese Americans to whom it belonged.

I happened to be the only Marine that was going through this training. All the rest were Navy and Army personnel, so there wasn't anyone in charge of me. They gave me what they called a "basket leave." I could write myself a leave and throw it in a basket as I went out the door and they would go over there and pick it up and check it. Well, I would take a basket leave whenever I could and head for the USO Club right there in Hollywood. I got to see all the famous movie stars that were in the area and I was able to meet them, actually talk to them and shake their hands. Later on in the war I saw a number of these stars in different shows over in the South Pacific. Bob Hope, Ray Milland and big, big stars came over and there would be thousands of men sitting around. I thought I had been pretty lucky to have seen them up close back in Hollywood. Those boys who were sitting on the hill would never get to count the freckles on Rita Hayworth.

Whatever time I wasn't spending at the USO, you would find me studying to see if I couldn't better myself. I think the Marine Corps did a good job training me.

SETTING SAIL

Every Marine at some point will get on a ship. It was my first time to be aboard a sea-going vessel when I boarded a freight ship in San Diego, California, that had been converted to a troop ship. At the end of the trip I wrote my mother: "Mom, I have just completed a 28-day cruise aboard a ship in the beautiful South Pacific. It was a slow, leisurely trip and many people became friends of mine as we changed course so many times we wondered if we were traveling in a circle."

We were actually on submarine watch twenty-four hours a day, and any floating debris or group of pelicans or other sea birds would cause bells to go off and this old ship would change directions. I was confused as to which way we were going because each time you looked for the sun it was on a different side of the ship.

Coming from the mid-west and not having been on a ship it's not surprising I got seasick. The trip was a lengthy thing and so I soon got over the seasickness. We went 28 days and 28 nights, zigzagging one way and then the other, crossing the equator about six times. We went to New Caledonia, the farthest point from home that I had ever been, 7,726 miles from Overton, Missouri.

I can remember thinking as we were sailing on that ship how I used to go down to the end of the road in Overton and sit along the river and take a look at the old Missouri floating by. And I would think, "Dang, if you had any kind of watercraft you could just shove it in here, in this river, and you could go anywhere in the world by this water. If you went down stream, then joined the Mississippi you could go right on out to the ocean." And here I was, out in that very ocean, zigzagging across the equator and it was quite an experience for an ole boy that grew up in a country store.

Having always been interested in carpentry, I watched the ship's carpenter working hard on one of the longest boards I had ever seen. I asked him, "Just what are you making?" He quickly answered, "I am making what they call a plank! Since we are traveling south – well, most of the time – when you cross the equator for the first time you are given the joy of walking the plank."

"Are you going to have to sand this long board for splinters from one end to the other?" was my next question. "Yes, because you always walk the plank barefooted."

The next day revealed a sight I could hardly believe. I was out for a stroll on the deck, taking advantage of the cruise the Marine Corps had so graciously provided me at no charge when I noticed the ship's carpenter had bolted the long plank to the deck at just about mid-ship, and extended it way out over the ocean. This wasn't just any board. It was the longest board I had ever seen in my life. It seemed like I had read about redwood trees being that long, but whatever it was, they had a huge long board. They'd get out there and sand on it all day long. I wondered if the Captain had asked them to make this for a submarine lookout. It looked so high that I hoped I would never be given that submarine watch station. If a person ever lost his balance, it would surely give him a jolt when he hit the water. Even the thought of such a thing happening made me wonder if there were little brown circles forming in the seat of my famous green-colored skivvies.

Every morning they'd take this plank out and anchor the base and hang it out over the rail, and if you were given the honor of walking the plank, why you would get up on there and they would blindfold you. You were barefoot so you would slide your feet ever so carefully as you took each step. They didn't have to tell you that part. If you went to the side, you would feel it and you could ease back on. Then when you would come to the end why, hell, you fell off. That was walking the plank. You literally fell off in the ocean.

We didn't know they had a way of turning that board around. They put you up on there while you were blindfolded and then they turned it around back to the center of the ship. Then they took off the top of the hatch and had a great big tank of water down below. They let you think you are walking that plank to your death and you'd get out there and fall off that thing and you'd go down in that tank. It was scary and everybody was hollering, "Man overboard! Man overboard!" They would ring bells and make a big ceremony out of it. I was selected to walk the plank two times. I talked to the captain about that, and when I asked why I had to walk the plank two times, he said, "Oh, we lost the records, I guess.

You know what, we crossed the equator before you got your certificate."
I said, "I didn't have a certificate." He said, "Well that's why you had to
walk the plank twice. If you can't produce that certificate you've got to
walk the plank again." So as we zigzagged across the ocean all those days,
I don't know how many times we crossed the equator, but I know I got to
walk the plank twice.

HANGING OUT OVER THE OCEAN

As we zigzagged across the ocean, I drew the job of helping fire the .50 caliber machine gun on the bow of the ship. Navy personnel manned that ship and the guns. We got to have a training session and the guy that pulled my target wanted to know, "Who's firing that .50 caliber on the bow?" They told him that I was the one. He said, "Well, don't lose sight of him. He just tore our target all to hell." So after that, they trusted me to stand watch with the Navy guys up on the bow.

The ship was so full of troops, there wasn't any place to sit or stand. We were standing submarine watch from the time we left San Diego all the way across.

It was bad that there was no place to sit and I didn't like that you had to go downstairs to sleep. It wasn't good. I had been issued a jungle hammock before we left to go overseas so I took it out and tied it to the turret on the bow of the ship where the machine gun was mounted, and I slept in my hammock tied to the machine gun off the side of the ship. When we'd get in rough seas, that hammock would actually swing out over the ocean and you could look down and see all that water below. Then it would swing back and very gently let you ease up against the side of the machine gun turret.

Some of the Navy personnel were standing watch and the captain came by on inspection and he looked at my hammock and he said, "Who in the hell is sleeping in that?" They replied "That silly Marine that's standing watch with us. Why did you ask?" The captain said, "Man, I want to see the guy that sleeps in there. You find out where he is and send him down to my quarters." So they came and found me and told me the captain wanted to see me. And I wondered what I had done now. It seemed like I was always skirting trouble. When I went down to see the captain he said, "I just want to see the guy that's sleeping in that hammock under that machine gun. What is wrong with you?" I said, "That's the best place on the ship, Captain. I don't have to look for a place to sit down. I can go lay down and zip that thing up and if it turns over I'm hoping the top will hold me." It had mosquito netting which you could zip to the hammock. If I flipped over I was sure hoping it was strong enough to hold me till somebody could get me out of there. It was quite an experience and I had a good visit with the captain.

GUADALCANAL AND BOUGAINVILLE

The first thing that we did when we were over in the Pacific was to stretch telephone line from one end of New Caledonia to the other and that's where I should have gotten my first purple heart. I took a hold of the corner post and when the boy I was working with pulled the line; he broke the post off and put me in the hospital. I fell right in front of a hospital jeep and they just reached over and picked me up and put me in the seat and took me to sickbay.

From there we went on to Guadalcanal, our permanent home for about seven periods of training in and out of the islands. The tents were up and stretched all the time. If you ever got back there, you had a place to sleep and to stay. It was kind of like a hotel away from home. We would leave this campsite for a period of time and go aboard ship. We would go to an island and then sail around it on standby, in case we were needed to help secure it. Sometimes we had to make the landing ourselves to secure the island. I was on standby for a number of islands and in between we would go back and train at our campsite on Guadalcanal. I made a total of four landings.

The first landing I made was on the island of Bougainville, in October of 1943. There was no feeling of loneliness like there was when we landed on that island. There were huge trees on Bougainville, I mean they were gigantic. Our job was to secure the island and to do that we cut down many of these trees. It was an experience to see trees that large, where the roots would grow way up, 40 feet in the air and join the trunk. There's a wilderness underneath that tree and snipers were of no threat there because no bullet could work its way through these huge tree trunks and root systems. Every night it rained and water pooled under the trees. You would sit down, lean against the trunk and sleep in the water. That's the way we slept on Bougainville.

One of the first things we did was to set up a camp by a mountain pass. There was a [Japanese] Zero that would come by every morning and strafe our chow line. We would get in line with our mess kits, and this guy would come down through those mountains and he'd shoot the road all up and kill a couple of guys. We would run to the big old trees and jump in the trees for cover. He did that day after day. We tried to kill him with our rifles but we just didn't have any luck.

Then radar came along. There were so many inventions during the war. They created ways to turn the ships upside down and work on them. There were new airplanes and speed boats for the Navy. Kaiser-Frazer took over and built ships. Everything was going on. It was a completely different world. Well, they decided that they had perfected the radar control of guns. A gun could now be fired by radar instead of a man pulling a trigger. They could shoot ships out at sea and they got it perfected to where they could shoot airplanes. I got to string the telephone line to the gun so we could shoot these planes as they flew across the island. They set a gun up to try to get this one in particular that kept strafing our chow line.

Boy, the next morning when he came through, it just disintegrated that plane. The ammunition aboard the airplane exploded and the pilot was scattered all over the road, all over the camp, all over us. Nobody could eat their chow that day. They just dumped their biscuits in the garbage and went back to what they were doing.

One day a group of Seabees from New Zealand and Australia landed and began clearing up the jungle and building roads. As I stood beside the clearing, a huge bulldozer passed me as it pushed one of the trees to the side. Then it made a beeline to where I was standing. This tremendous machine stopped and the operator yelled, "It's tea time, mate! Come on, I'm sharing."

He dropped his big steel blade to the earth hard and we both sat behind it, as sniper bullets ricocheted off of the blade. We stayed in this spot for about 30 minutes. It wasn't long before we knew each other's name, age, where we were from, and what we liked. Then I was introduced to what Limeys talk and sing about and wish for during tea time. Before leaving, I knew he had jolly sixpence and something to send home to his wife, poor wife. We had a nice visit and then I headed back to my campsite.

As I walked back to our communication center I was thinking this had not been such a bad maneuver after all. On my way, I saw a shortcut that looked inviting. I decided to check it out because it was a good, clean-looking trail. I got about 30 feet down the path and I stepped into a trench and fell through a layer of brush that was spread over the trail, camouflaging the bamboo pit below. It was not real deep but I managed to get a shallow wound on my shin that bled and burned like fire.

It didn't seem so bad, so I put a bandage on it and returned to the trail I never should have strayed from.

The captain had told us it would be a short landing and it was. We had orders to return to Guadalcanal. I decided to report to sick bay before I went aboard ship and when the doctor saw my leg he sent me on a plane to Guadalcanal to be a patient at the Army hospital there. He didn't tell me, but I have always thought he knew right then I had blood poisoning. I sure didn't like the large lumps that had developed under each arm and the big lumps I had on each side of my groin. A bumpy old plane ride is never a pleasure, but it was good, to know that as soon as this was over I would be back at my camp and be able to join the rest of my comrades.

This wasn't my first chance to learn you shouldn't make plans for the next day when you are in the Marines. I was sent directly to the large base hospital on Guadalcanal. The next day my captain was at the hospital bright and early, and after talking to the staff he came to visit me. He made no bones about my condition. I had stepped into a poisoned bamboo splint pit and he told me that he was going to call Los Angeles and have a doctor friend of his catch a plane to Guadalcanal. That sure made me feel I was in the best outfit there was.

Three days the doctor stayed. First he took a great big needle and gave me a shot of penicillin. Everyday for all the time I was in that hospital, I took that same shot of penicillin. After cutting my wound open, they scraped the bone and then put my leg in traction. The big old weight they put on the end of it was so heavy it would pull me right out of bed. If you turned loose of the top of the bed, down to the foot you'd go. It was too much weight, but that's the way they wanted it.

At the end of the third day he said, "I have to get back to my hospital, but I have been here long enough to know who the best corpsman is and he will take over my job and be in charge of you from now on." For 28 days I lay in this position as they poured very hot water, followed by cold water, on a huge pack of towels wrapped around my leg. 24 hours a day for all those 28 days. They saved me from having to have that leg amputated. It's kind of a scary thing to think about, even now. War conditions never seem to allow you to say the proper thanks, so I am going to now say "Thank You!" to all the corpsmen, doctors, nurses and families who helped us and saved many of our lives.

HILLBILLIES AND A HOLLYWOOD ACTOR

Taking Cpl. Krohn's advice, I chose Sy Miller as my buddy. Sy was possibly the greatest choice I could have made. He was from a small community like me — Goose Creek, Tennessee. Perhaps the sling shot that was always hanging from his rear dungaree pocket influenced me the most, for I always enjoyed shooting one. He was the best shot I had ever seen. He would place the handle in his left hand and stretch rubber with his right and shoot a projectile through the air and send any bird plummeting to the earth, no matter how high the tree.

One night I was Sergeant of the Guard when we were at camp on Guadalcanal, and it was my job to see that all lights were turned off at 10 o'clock. I had yelled for a Master Sergeant to turn off his light and probably wasn't putting enough authority in my voice to receive the proper action. When I said, "I'm going to have to get out of bed and go down there and help my Master Sergeant turn his light off," Sy said, "Wait a minute," and reached down under his cot. He took out his sling shot, picked up a rock, and shot out the light bulb two tents down the line. The shattering of glass was the last sound I heard that night and there was never a word said about it.

Sy was the kind of person you would like to be if you were a young Marine. He had a quick smile that showed his right front tooth was made out of gold. He is the Marine I think about more than any other and I will always remember him. Until the day he died, I put my full trust in him, and each day that I spent in the service afterward, I missed him!

The word had gotten out that Marine Corpsman Robert (Bob) Webber was an entertainer and had worked as an extra in movies. So it was only a matter of time before he was signed up to appear in one of the U.S.O. shows. Bob was really into the entertainment profession and carried all kinds of props and uniforms in his seabag.

I still remember the first time I ever saw him perform on stage. After being invited to join the show, he simply pulled out a huge, over-sized sweater that he and another performer both got into, one standing behind the other. The sweater had four sleeves which made it possible for them to get on a stage and make it appear as if it were one really large man attempting to do things. It is hard to believe that the two of them could entertain a large crowd of battle-weary Marines simply by scratching their butt with four hands or rearranging their privates which were never in the proper position. They even had a nose-picking routine with all four hands, which caused a lot of shouting and yelling and clapping by the young men who were so glad to get out of fighting and enjoy some laughter together.

I couldn't believe it when Bob joined my forward observer team for Naval Gunfire two days later. When he introduced himself by saying, "Hi, my name is Robert Webber" — his name was nothing special to me. After a couple of years in the South Pacific that name took on a special meaning and generated both respect and recognition.

The Captain of our company had a rule that if you were a sergeant or above, you could go to our motor pool and check out a vehicle, even for recreational use. I took advantage of this rule many times, and I can remember Bob talking me into requesting a four-wheeler for the day, and taking him to the other end of Guadalcanal to visit a young woman. She was on the island with a U.S.O. show and had worked with him when he was an extra in Hollywood. It was a great day to sit among so many men who held such great rank and just listen to the conversations and see such a wonderful sight as a beautiful actress from Hollywood who seemed to draw officers like flies on buttermilk. It was several years later when I went to see the movie "The Dirty Dozen," in which Bob acted that I truly understood how much respect he deserved. I also enjoyed seeing him in many television shows, like "The Twilight Zone."

TESTING THE LANDING STRIP

One day on Bougainville I really didn't have anything to do, so I was goofing off. I found an opening that would let you go down and stand and see about a mile of beach. It was the prettiest sight that you could ever want to see. It seemed like there hadn't been anybody around. Then I got to looking up the beach and there was something going on, so I thought I'd go check it out. When I got real close to the activities, I came out of the trees onto the beach.

It turned out they were making a temporary landing strip for the fighter planes so they could come off the aircraft carriers and land on the island. They had brought in steel matting and laid it on the sand for what looked like a mile. It was a pretty wide strip, and it all hooked together.

They were in the process of testing the landing strip and when they brought in the first plane, I was right there. The pilot attempted to land on that steel matting. He went about 40 or 50 feet, that's all the further he got because it began to buckle up in front of his airplane. It buckled so much that his propeller cut into it and it tore the propeller off. Then the plane nosed over and just tumbled on down the landing strip. The pilot was killed instantly, of course, and they just drug his plane off and took the bulldozer and stretched that thing back out. Then they called for another plane to land. They didn't attempt to anchor it or do anything about the fact that it had buckled. They just pulled it back, stretched it out with their equipment and in came another plane. When the plane went by, I was so close I had a view of the cockpit. I never saw a man sitting so rigid in my life and have such a tight grip as he had on that stick that he was holding. You could just tell that he was tense and he died the same way. That plane tumbled and it took a half an hour to get it cleaned up. They stretched it out again and then they brought the third one in and I thought, "God, how many times are they going to try this? It's not working. Two is enough." But in came another one and I could see the fear in his face, and he tumbled, too. They didn't have it anchored and it just wasn't staying and it would buckle and scoot and get up in the props. Still, they sent a fourth guy in, and he too had a tight hold on that wheel. Just then I thought, "Oh this is it. When he makes contact it will start to peel up," But he just pulled back on the stick and went RAOOOOOOOOO-OOOOOOMMMMMMMMMMMMMM, like that, and he did a circle and come down and landed in the ocean. He climbed out and walked on to the wing. There were Navy personnel running all around and a Higgins boat went out to pick him up. They took him off that wing and they didn't send any more airplanes in. I think he probably saved a lot of lives that day. I don't know how long they would have run those pilots in there. An airplane and a pilot that's trained; what a costly thing to waste.

SUNDAY DRIVE

Another time when we were stationed at Noumea, New Caledonia, I was taking several people on what I was told was an information trip. I was quite happy to be on this adventure in a four-wheel drive vehicle. The driver convinced us that this road had been driven before. He had seen it on one of our military maps so we were enjoying a lovely Sunday afternoon drive. We came upon what appeared to be a clearing in the coconut grove and our road turned into a couple of tracks. No one challenged our driver or even asked any questions about whether he knew where he was going. As the two tracks seemed to take on a slight curve, our vehicle leaned and you had to exert a great deal of pressure against the person sitting beside you. This made me think of my younger days, when I would take my girlfriend on such a drive and look for a road like this. She could almost be sitting in your lap and never complain as she thought you were just trying to keep her in the truck.

I then became engrossed in memories of my brother and how a small fight might start from a situation like this. I was thinking how much I would rather be there than where I was on this Sunday afternoon, I was actually longing for such a fight, dreaming of how hard I was going to hit my brother, when there was a sudden change of scenery. Ahead burst forth a waterfall in a mountain stream that was approximately 20 feet high. This waterfall fell into a large swimming hole that nature lovers only dream of finding. The truck had barely come to a stop before there were six piles of clothes along the road. At the end of those six piles stood six men, naked as jay birds, shouting "Last one in is a ____!" The blank can be filled in with any of the derogatory remarks known in the Marine Corps vocabulary.

These memories allow me to get away from fighting the war and remind me that there were many days that were enjoyable.

CATCHING UP WITH SAM

Things went along very well and I received packages from home. We had a colorful, lightweight paper that we called V-mail and I would write letters to my family quite regularly to keep in contact. I still had it in my mind to get caught up with my brother, Sam, who was by then serving in the 3rd Division of the Marine Corps. After the five Sullivan brothers, who were all members of the same unit, had died at the same time, the President of the United States didn't want two people from the same family in the same outfit. But if you could get one of your parents to write a letter of intention, they would make an exception. So I asked my mother and she wrote the letter and signed it. I carried that letter until I caught up with Sam on Guadalcanal, which was about a year and a half later.

In the spring of 1944, while I was stationed on Guadalcanal, I got a phone call one morning and they said, "We have made arrangements for you to join your brother. Pack your seabag and go out to the road and sit there until we get a 6 X 6 troop truck over there to pick you up." Well, about three hours later, after I'd sat there in the dust from all the cars and trucks that went by, here came a great big 6 X 6. I threw my seabag in there and jumped up in the truck and they took me to his campsite.

After I joined my brother, he became my officer in charge. I enjoyed that. He was quite a radioman and good with Morse code. I was never too sharp on that. I did better with the telephone when somebody was on the other end to talk to. I often wondered why I was so slow sending Morse code, but I think it was just that there was no way for you to know if they were receiving the message. It didn't click for me like it did for my brother, so I became a telephone man.

Sam and I were together in the Third Marine Division when we made the landing on Guam. The landing spot was horrible, a rock cliff we couldn't get up. There was no way; no rope ladders we could use to climb, nothing. We lost a lot of men in the Third Division that day. Not only on the cliffs, but also in Higgins boats as they came into the beach. The men were floating all over the water and the boats were running through them and they were trying to swim away and boats were running over them.

It just wasn't going right for us at first. We couldn't climb straight up a rock cliff with all our gear. So we looked around and found a draw that we could use to get above those cliffs. After that the terrain was such that we could run. And we were running all day long, moving from one point to another, just run, run, run. We went almost three miles. We overtook their barracks and their central office, took the entire island before nightfall.

Sam had been a short order cook and he was a pretty good cook. He knew how to make hamburgers and fry everything there was to fry. He made a good brain sandwich and all kinds of special stuff. One day after our landing on Guam, Sam found this saw blade at an old saw mill that was all torn up. This saw blade was just laying there and Sam suggested we take it back to camp. And I said, "That thing? You can't carry that. If you drop it, it'll tear your foot off." That thing was heavy and at least four foot in diameter. He started looking around and found an axel that looked like it had come out of an old car. He stuck it through the hole in the middle of the blade and then the guys could put it on their shoulders and could walk along. It was so heavy you had to have four men to move it. We got it back to camp and he got to making hotcakes. Sam got in with the cook and got him to order hotcake mix. The cook would invite all the high brass people around there who he wanted to make friends with to come down to eat hotcakes with Sam. It kept growing and growing and it got to where you couldn't get any hotcakes there were so many people standing around with their mess kits. That whole saw blade would be covered with hotcakes. They had a time. They carried that thing back and forth from one campsite to another. He got to be a very famous cook for his Saw Blade Hotcakes.

During the few months that Sam and I were together in combat, I went though something very difficult. We had finished setting up our communications center close to the trees and I needed to relieve myself. I stepped about ten feet into the wooded area, thinking it was always better to be in the woods when you wanted to take a leak. There seemed to be a great deal of noise of all types as if troops were advancing, and while I was wondering why this was, a Japanese soldier only eight feet away got up on one knee with a Molotov cocktail in his hand. There was no doubt that his target was our radio jeep.

I had no choice but to fire my weapon, and I can remember saying to myself, "He is only a young boy!" Even though I was not through urinating, reflex action took over and I pulled the trigger. I was trained beyond my control. As my first shot rang out several other shots followed.

I remember thinking, "We don't know who killed him!" And I seemed to comfort myself with that thought. But it was still so upsetting to me. Every time before that, I'd heard a lot of other shots and never felt I was the one. But this time I was so close that I knew I would have to take the blame for killing that man.

A Major, who was driving by, stopped and said, "I'll get rid of him." The Major jumped out of his jeep and threw a rope around the dead man's neck, and as he started with a jerk the young man's tongue was forced way out of his mouth. I shouted for the Major to stop, I walked out and lowered the rope to his arm pits and yelled "O.K.!" The major drove away as I tried to console myself. Nothing helped me more than to simply say, "God knows who killed him." Sam showed up right after that and he asked me what happened, but I didn't tell him. There were plenty of other things to talk about.

I can remember one day an old Japanese man came crawling in on his hands and knees. He had elephantitis. They took him and put him in the guard barracks where they had a prisoner fence and he just sat there. I guarded that guy for my four hours. He looked pitiful, and it was just a thing that was so hard to watch. Then the fellow that followed me took over and about two hours into his guard duty, I heard a shot. I went running over there and asked what happened. He said, "He ran." I thought, Yeah, he ran. He couldn't even walk in here. You know there was no way he could run out. He got tired of guarding him is what happened. Combat will cause you to do odd, odd things. There's no end to the things you will do.

I still remember Sam's colonel. He was well liked and I was with him when the first P-38 I ever saw came flying over. It was obvious that the man who was flying that plane was drunk as he could be. He flew under all the bridges that the engineers had put across the river and he flew under telephone lines and almost touched the ground. The colonel got so irate that he yelled, "Shoot him down! Shoot him down!! The next time he comes across fire your weapon at him and see if we can get him down. He's going to kill a bunch of our men. The plane is twice as important as he is, but we are going to have to put an end to it." I shot at him, but I made damn sure I didn't hit him. That P-38 was something. Built by Lockheed, this fighter aircraft literally changed the war. We had all we could do to fight the air battles with that old Grumman and here was this super fast P-38 that could run circles around that old Mustang they were flying. We had good pilots and they got kills and credit for shooting down airplanes, but we did not have air superiority at that time. With these new planes came a need for pilots and Sam got the opportunity to go for training. He came up to the front and talked to me and asked, "What do you think I should do? Do you think I should stick it out here or should I go?" I had just killed the first man I had ever killed in my life, and when he asked me that question I said, "If I were in your shoes I'd be getting out of here right now. I wouldn't even wait here and talk to me. I'd go." He said: "I kind of expected you would say that, but I just had to hear it before I left." While I hated to see him go, I knew we would need good pilots to win this war.

Sam and I were only together for a short time. When he left that was the last time I saw him during the war. He shipped out and went back to his company and got his orders from his colonel who he had been with ever since he had joined the Marines. His colonel was almost 70 years old, and that's like an old grandpa in the Marines. He liked Sam and Sam liked him, and he helped Sam move up through the ranks.

Sam became a good pilot. I particularly remember one story told to me about him and an officer buddy who had planned to bear hunt near one of our bases. Sam convinced his buddy that he was a good enough pilot to scout for bear from his helicopter. He said he was only trying to get close enough to make sure that old grizzly was a male when he flew his helicopter too close to a fir tree. He ended up clipping off a bunch of limbs and had to land in a farmer's field. He was up for advancement to Major at the time and had to pay the farmer for all eight acres in the field or he was told he would be bypassed for advancement. So the only real enjoyment he got was driving out to the farmer's field and watching the farmer combine the beans that he had paid for. The bear hunt never came off, and I imagine there might have been two wives behind that decision, since the bear scouting had surely cut into their budget.

Sam eventually became a flight deck officer on an aircraft carrier. During his career in the Marines, he would become a well-known pilot and at one time was flying the largest helicopter in the Marines and teaching other pilots to fly them. He was so skilled he was chosen to be the Marine Pilot in charge of setting the lantern room on top of the Oak Island lighthouse at Cape Fear, North Carolina.

TASTY TREATS

Jungle rations were a real treat, especially the ones with beans and franks. But I can't say anything good about the left-over rations we got from World War I. It was strong, strong mutton. That was rough, just a hard way to go. But back to pork and beans, they were such an important part of our diet that one morning while we were in brigade formation we had a ceremony honoring Mr. Van Camp. This crazy Tech Sergeant wanted to give him the Medal of Honor for inventing pork and beans and single handedly saving the Marine Corps in the South Pacific. The way he had written it was really a piece of work, and it was lots of fun.

It was hard to beat a can of pork and beans and if you could get to a PX and get you a can of pork and beans, that was living. I hope I don't get arrested for telling you this, but when we landed on Guam our Forward Observer team had a jeep. I decided to take the extra radio out of the jeep and bury it and then I headed over to the PX and got me a case of pork and beans and I put it down in where the extra radio belonged and locked it up and I carried a key to it.

After we were ashore, my rear-wheel drive went out and all I had was front-wheel drive. I went all over that island throwing mud. I mean I could throw mud even if it hadn't rained for two days. It was hard to get along and I would slip and slide without that rear-wheel drive. I got to thinking, "Man. I'm going to get stopped by an MP and he'll probably make me take it off the road." I was holding people up and they were trying to get around me and honking. I was handicapped and I knew it. I tried to stay in my line and stay with my company. Then I heard a siren coming, "Hell, I'll try and outrun 'em," and I opened that thing up and was going down the road, driving it hard, and they just kept gaining on me, blowing the siren. Finally I just stopped, pulled over, got out and put my hands in the air. I couldn't outrun them with nothing but front-wheel drive. Lucky for me the guy that was chasing me was that nut that had written the piece about Mr. Van Camp. He said, "What the hell's wrong with you?" I said, "Boy, am I glad to see you. I don't like the two MPs I see with you, but I'm glad to see you." He said, "These are buddies of mine. We want a can of pork and beans." I let them have all the beans they wanted, and was sure glad it was just that fellow and his buddies.

When mail call happened over in the South Pacific I sometimes got a fruitcake from my sister, Marie. She would buy these great big six pound fruit cakes and they would come in a pasteboard box and she would mail them to me. When I got one there was a trail of people that would follow me back to my tent and we'd break open a knife and we'd cut that thing. You wouldn't figure on saving any of it because there was a stream of people and the cake was gone when you quit cutting. So you'd better be eatin' while you're cuttin' or you wouldn't get any. That's the way it was.

I had a buddy, Vandorhn, who I had trained with and we'd been together on a number of landings. Whenever he got around fruit he had a habit of making apple jack. He got real drunk one time and he woke me up in the middle of the night. He said, "Sarge? Sarge?" And he couldn't talk plain at all. I asked what was the matter, and if he was hurt. No, he wasn't hurt. He got sick, real sick and went down to the latrine and when he threw up he lost his partial. He said, "My three front teeth are down there in the latrine. I've got to have those teeth. I can't make it without them. Come help me find them." So I got my flashlight and we went down there and he showed me where he was sitting and everything. And I'm holding the light and he looked down and saw them. And I said, "Well, we found them. Now it's up to you to get them out!" He said, I'll get them out, but I'll kill you if you ever tell anybody about this!"

FORWARD OBSERVATIONS

When they formed the 6th Marine Division in September, 1944, the Joint Assault Signal Unit needed telephone men. So I made my application and they came and got me and started training me as a forward observer. A forward observer radios to the people aboard ship way out in the ocean and then they fire the guns where you tell them to. It was a huge responsibility. Many times you really wondered if you were doing the right thing. The officer would give you a target and then you worked out the coordinates. The guns we were firing were so big that if we got within 200 yards it was considered a direct hit. If you were off a little bit, it would not only blow you up, but blow up everybody else within 200 yards. When those big guns go off, by the time you heard the blast, it was already past you and exploded. There wasn't a chance to rectify what you had done. Then you sit and look with your binoculars and you say, "Up 200 yards," or, "Right 200 yards," in whatever direction you want them to move. That was your job as forward observer and you were responsible for many, many a person. Sometimes, on those little islands over there, when the shells were going over your head, you would think it was going to jerk your helmet off. You would wonder, "Boy, did I do it now? Did I get it too low?" But if it worked out and you hit your target there was kind of a joy, and the experience made you thankful that you could do this kind of thing. I would hesitate today to take hold of such a responsibility. I don't think I could handle it.

As a forward observer, even though I was a member of the Marine Corps, I was technically a member of the Navy and under their jurisdiction. They do that because they don't want to have forward observers telling people to fire a mission without being a part of Navy personnel. So I got to know the Navy guys that fired the guns. It was important to go out and meet the man who is going to be talking to you on the radio when you fire a mission. The man I worked with from the battleship Pennsylvania said, "If I know some way of identifying you and I can be sure you are who you say you are, I can fire that mission much quicker and it might save lives." If they knew you, they would feel better about firing a mission for you. So they would let me go aboard ship and visit. I'd always try to talk them out of a big old dish of ice cream, because we couldn't get any when we were on the islands.

Even though I was a Marine, I was under the jurisdiction of the Navy and they were in charge of my seabag. Well, they managed to lose it on three different occasions. Seemed like they were always losing my seabag. While they said I was attached to the Navy, I wasn't sure if I was attached to the Navy or just detached from everybody.

When you come back to your home base and your seabag is missing, you've lost everything, your clothes, all your records, your mailing addresses, your Bible, everything. You would get it back eventually, but it sure did mess you up while it was gone. I did carry a picture of my girlfriend, Jan, and a little Bible in my shirt pocket the whole time I was overseas.

I got to go aboard the flagship one day and see Admiral Halsey. I was lucky I guess in a way to come from a little old town and see the many men who are now in storybooks, who took command of the Marine Corps. Something about being a forward observer is that those in command don't want you out of their sight. You are their boy, you know. "Where's my Forward Observer?" And they'd treat the AGL [Air Guard Liaison] the same way. You didn't wander off very far, because they'd be hollering for you. And when they went somewhere, you went too. If they did something, they wanted this group to be with them. Kind of like the movie stars do. They were leaders and they wanted to have a bunch of people around them all the time. It was quite an experience.

NATIVE AMERICAN MARINES

We had several Native Americans in the Marine Corps, many of whom were code talkers. Also known as wind talkers, these Indians, by using their own language, could freely communicate and exchange important information without fear of being understood by the Japanese. Throughout the war, the Japanese were never able to break their "code." The wind talkers were always near the headquarters of every unit. Because of their dark hair and complexion they could easily be mistaken for Japanese and needed protection.

I particularly remember a Native American captain that I got to know, and I will always respect the wisdom he used in dealing with his men. He was a favorite leader among the Marines at that time, and I was attached to his unit as their forward observer. We were out on maneuvers and he said to his men, "You know, Indians have got to have meat. We're meat eaters, and these C-Rations just don't get it. I'm gonna have one of the guys shoot me a dove. And I'm gonna call a halt and set down and I'm gonna get me a stick and I'm gonna cook that dove and I'm going to eat the whole thing, you know. I'm just gonna get me some meat." So they shot, shot, shot, finally one of the guys got a dove. The captain stopped the whole group to 'Fall out.' And they crapped out. I mean they were ready for a rest. So he sat there and he held that bird over that fire till it was burned to a crisp. I said, "You gonna ruin your dove holding it so close to the flame." He said, "The dove is not important."

I asked, "Well, why in the world did you have them shoot the dove? You should have had me shoot the limb out from under it and let the fall kill it." He laughed really hard. He thought that was funny. It wouldn't have been all shot up. Hell, that old 30 caliber just about exploded its body and he didn't have much to cook. He said, "The cooking is not what's important."

I said, "Well then, tell me what is important if you are going to eat that dove?" He said, "I'm going to eat that dove, no matter how dry and hard it gets. I'm killing time. Don't you realize how tired my men are? If we were to have an attack right now I'd lose at least half my men. We are dead tired. They are as tired as they can be and they've got to have some rest, and the only way they're gonna get it is to call a halt and make them crap out. My men are the most important thing."

He told me he was glad to have me with him. He was grateful that Naval gunfire had recently shot two holes in a big, tall tower the Japanese had been using for sniper fire and brought an end to it. His conversation was worth a great deal to me. And he even gave me a small bite of that overcooked dove.

When I try to remember some of the great things about him, the most significant thing seems to be that anytime we were on patrol during the dark hours of the night, he always wore Indian moccasins and could walk without making a sound. They were life saving equipment!

THE FLOATING DOLLAR BILL

My entire forward observer team will have to be a part of this story, when we were on standby for an amphibious landing in the South Pacific around the island of Peleliu. We had been aboard this ship for several days to see if we would be sent ashore for the battle, and it seemed like every meal had been a canteen cup full of navy bean soup. This was a particularly good excuse for a swim party. At least it was a legitimate way of saying to all the Marines aboard, "Get off my ship and let it air out!"

Some maneuvering was required to get the ship in position, but as soon as the rope ladders were thrown overboard there followed a scampering of Marines down them, ready for a good saltwater swim and some fresh air. Sleeping head to toe, the way we did on that hot troop ship, we needed a breath of fresh air, too.

They put a bunch of swabbies along the rail with rifles to keep the sharks off of us while we were swimming. I was enjoying the swim but it did not last long. The submarines following us began a maneuver with the intention of interrupting our swim party. Sirens started blaring — bells were ringing, signal flares were exploding, and every sailor in the convoy was yelling "Submarine attack!" And every man in the swim party was swimming as fast as he could toward the rope ladders — except for one Marine.

This Marine had spied a floating one dollar bill which was folded in such a manner that it seemed to be holding his head in its hands and leisurely bobbing along. As it floated past me, it seemed to sing its own song, "Catch me if you can! Catch me if you can!"

I was just about to reach for the rope ladder when a voice inside me said, "You really should get that dollar bill." My decision to become a dollar richer was a great mistake, for at that instant our Captain gave the order "Engage prop," in an attempt to gain attack position for defense of a submarine. The first turn of the prop seemed to lurch our ship to one side, and I thought, "Okay, forget the dollar bill!!" But as I reached out to grab the landing net, the changing of the ship's position had caused the net to swing way out from the port side and I was going to be drawn into the undertow caused by one giant propeller.

I was swimming as fast and as hard as I possibly could and soon realized that it was a losing battle. I looked at that big old prop and I thought, "I'll never make it." So I started saying my prayers and telling my family goodbye. And as I began to face this reality I went into an out-of-body experience. It felt as if I were no longer in control and seemed to be in contact with Mom and I was standing in a cemetery. The neighbor family had lost a baby girl and I was one of four young pallbearers. And my mother was saying, "They are having a closed casket funeral because the baby choked to death and turned so black. I hope I never have to have a closed casket funeral in our family." This made me wonder how many pieces the prop would chop my body into as the undertow fed me through. And it seemed that all I could say to her was, "I'm sorry, Mom! I used poor judgment and if I had another chance I would surely put a different value on a one dollar bill."

And then the prop stopped spinning and there was an AGL (Air Ground Liason) Lieutenant at the bottom of the rope ladder who had seen what had happened and knew the trouble I was in. He had climbed down that rope ladder from the fantail. What a great feeling it was when his hand made contact with mine and like a grip of steel he locked around my wrist and didn't let go until he saw both my hands hurriedly climbing to safety.

In the past it was with envy I watched the officers who I saw on the fantail aboard a troop ship with their alcohol highballs and lounge chairs. After that day I was happy to see officers relaxed and enjoying their down time, for they certainly had earned it. The Lieutenant's action that day won my admiration and respect.

BURYING THE DEAD

During the war there were soldiers who refused to carry a weapon. They were called COs, which stood for Conscientious Objectors. The COs in our outfits weren't too popular during my tour of duty. Among this group there were so many that deserve the greatest "Thank You!" I am able to bring forth. They carried no weapons, did not chase after the enemy soldiers, but rather chose to do everything in their power and training to make each casualty as comfortable as they could be.

Few of them ever received the thanks they deserved.

These corpsmen were some of the bravest Marines I ever knew. They would carry water to the men at the frontlines. Can you imagine heading out there with nothing but water and stopping at every man? It was also their job to help bury our dead. I thought, "Well, if I could do this with them, I could help some mother get one of these boys home." So I started helping out.

We would get on a wagon and ride, and when we come to a dead person they would jump off and start talking to him. My first question to the work crew was, "How come the first thing you do is say 'Hello!' to the Marine you are going to bury?" The reply was, "Each one of these men is a comrade, but we aren't acquainted with them. The only way I can know his name is to have his dog tag in my hand. We talk to them like their family would and we button their buttons, tie their shoes and put their helmets on straight. We do it to honor their mother because we feel that is something she would do if she could. Just continue to work with us and maybe we will be able to explain it."

Two days were long enough to keep me from asking any more questions. You did the things you were taught to do. We took the bolt out of their weapons and deposited it in an area where the enemy couldn't find it. We took our time with the men and buried them just a short distance under the surface of the earth, in a temporary grave. We fixed their bayonet, pushed it slowly down into the ground, feeling the top of his helmet as it scraped against the bayonet. This marked the exact spot where a fallen comrade could be retrieved. Then they might say, "Goodbye, Mom! Dad! And Family! We hope you are able to bring — home," and you say the name of the boy you have just buried. Dog tags are so small, and yet they contain so much information.

Many of these were temporary graves but not all. Some bodies were shipped home, but there are many cemeteries all over and dedicating them is another thing you have to learn to go through when you're in the Marine Corps. As I stood at attention and listened to taps being played at my first dedication of a cemetery, I made a promise that I would continue to help with the dead as long as I was able. It's a hard, hard thing to live through and every year you think about that on Veterans' Day. I stood at the dedication of many cemeteries in the South Pacific Islands, where the white crosses stretched as far as your eyes could see.

One day when we were in a brigade formation, after I had been released from the hospital, I heard my name called out, "Sergeant Oscar F. Oerly, front and center." I got out of rank and marched up there and saluted and said, "Sergeant Oerly reporting sir, as requested." I was thinking, "Gee, what'd I do now?" They began reading this long citation for service above and beyond the call of duty. That's when I realized I was getting a Bronze Star for helping the corpsmen with the death wagon. That was sure a surprise to me.

If there's anything I can do with this story, it's to say thank you to the people who were Conscientious Objectors who joined the Marine Corps and volunteered to be corpsmen. They are some of the heroes that I feel have never been given enough credit. No honor, no glory and I think there are a lot of people to this day that don't understand the part they played. If a person's got Conscientious Objector on his discharge papers, it might mean he is a coward to some, but to the ones he helped, he was a hero.

CHARLES B. PEARSON FROM PLANO, TEXAS

In September of 1944 the 6th Marine Division was formed for the Battle of Okinawa. I was part of a Joint Assault Signal Unit, as they needed telephone and radio men. I got my orders to report to the Sixth JASU.

One of the greatest leaders that I have ever had is Charlie Pearson. He joined the Assault Signal Unit and became my lieutenant and taught me a lot of things, most importantly how to be a fairly good forward observer in the Marine Corps. He taught me things that I didn't know about Naval gunfire and how to fire a mission. Another thing we learned to do was to light up the sky. We could call for flares from battleships out at sea and when we were under banzai attacks we could light up the night and sometimes this was the most effective thing we were able to do. It drove people wild to have the enemy charging at them in the dark. There you were, trying to get the bayonet on your weapon and they were already on top of you. So instead of fighting in the dark, we fought with plenty of light. It's not nearly as scary when you have someone coming at you screaming, "BANZAI!" if you can see them.

Once, while clearing the area for the night, we had one of these Banzai attacks come up. Pearson told me to crank up the generator so we could radio the ship to fire some flares. I was on the generator, sitting there and above us was a path that went up over the hill. I heard Pearson right above me make a funny noise and I knew something was wrong because you didn't hear much from Pearson. About the time I looked up he fired three real quick shots and this guy fell right on me before I could even get off the generator. Pearson said: "Don't move. The guy was about to throw a Molotov cocktail and he might still have it on him. Just sit there and be as still as you can until daylight." We didn't dare turn on our flashlights or light a match, as any little light could cause you to get killed. It was actually less than two hours until dawn, but it felt like two weeks. You have no concept of time on a night like that. It was one of the slowest nights I ever lived through.

CLOSE CALLS

Before each amphibious landing, I was always issued a jeep and it was a vital part of our equipment. There was a case made of steel on each side of the back seat of the jeep. Each case held the best communication radio available for combat, and deserved the greatest care a person could give it.

We had lost our jeep driver when we were involved in the landing on Guam. Our lieutenant had insisted our jeep driver be replaced, because it is almost impossible to send messages on your radio and drive at the same time. When our jeep driver replacement arrived, we were back on Guadalcanal training for the landing on Okinawa. Our new driver was a Jewish boy from the East Coast. When I asked him if he was a good jeep driver, he smiled and said, "Sure! Want to see my license?" He was a pleasant young man and it seemed that things were going to work out rather well.

The Corps of Engineers had built a bridge across the largest river on Guadalcanal; it consisted of three sets of pilings driven into the ground and timbers fastened to them. Then they used what looked like railroad ties to support runway boards set the proper distance apart. Using this bridge would save a number of miles over the old road and its low water bridge across the river.

I thought it was rather odd when our driver stopped the jeep and asked the question, "Do you want me to drive across the bridge?" And after saying, "Yes, I do!" I wished I had taken the time to look at his license. Everything was going OK until the driver seemed to get worried as to whether the front wheel on the right side of the jeep was running in the center of the timber plank. And as he tried to look and make certain it was, the tires ran off the runway boards and we hit about four big bumps between the cross ties before we vaulted into the river below.

The water seemed very cold for the island temperature to be so warm. I was starting to relax and enjoy it as I sat in cool running water keeping my microphone in the dry so I could complete my message. When I looked, our radio jeep was upside down in the middle of the river with all four wheels still spinning as if it were trying to say, "I'll give you all I can." But it didn't matter how many times those tires turned, that jeep was going nowhere.

Another close call involved Jim Dietrich an AGL (Air Ground Liaison) I served with in the 6th Marine Division. Our campsite was in a coconut grove. We had a washstand outside the tent and that's where we shaved. We were getting fired at every once in awhile, so I wanted to wear my helmet and borrowed my friend Jim Dietrich's to use as a basin. There's a liner in the helmet that will hold water. Jim was sitting there on his cot talking and laughing as I was shaving. All of a sudden I got hit in the head by a coconut, and I turned around and there's a boy sitting there with a couple of coconuts in his hand and I thought he'd thrown that coconut at me while I was shaving. That coconut hit me so hard it might have killed me if I'd not been wearing my helmet. Well, I was going to fix him. I was going to beat him up. I had every intention of fighting that guy. Jim came running out of the tent hollering, "No, no, Sarge! Wait a minute!" He grabbed a hold of me 'cause I was going after that boy that had the coconuts. He said, "That guy didn't throw that coconut at you! It came out of the tree. I watched it fall down and hit you in the head." It was a good thing he stopped me!

Your helmet could be the difference between life and death. We had a Sergeant Major that would always yell and scream if he saw a man with no helmet on. Then one night he didn't wear his, and on the way to the latrine he got shot right between the eyes. For all the yelling he did and then to die that way sure didn't seem right.

CRABS, WORMS AND TOAD FROGS

While we had our training camp on Guadalcanal, we were overrun by sea crabs several times. They would come out of the ocean and their prehistoric route was right through the middle of our camp. There was nothing we could do to disrupt this route. They were determined to make the same trip they always had to lay their eggs and then return to the ocean.

The second time they attacked, our captain had trenches dug around our camp. Then he had an ample supply of kerosene added to the trenches and burned the crabs as they crossed. The smell of scorched crabs was so bad it caused everyone to vomit and no one could continue with the "seafood barbeque."

The flies were just horrible on Guam. While we buried our own dead every morning, the enemy bodies were just laying around. This island also had more than its fair share of toad frogs. They were just as thick as they could be and they'd climb up on the bodies and eat so many flies that their bellies would burst right open and draw more flies.

About a day before we left aboard ship to go to Okinawa, they came by and sprayed all of our clothing. They had discovered a worm in the streams on the island that would get on you like a leech and penetrate the skin and then go inside your bloodstream and create a very serious situation. So they sprayed all our clothing and it set up in the cloth. When you went to take your clothes off, why you could just stand them in the corner because they were nothing but stiff. You can't really imagine what that spray would do to a pair of pants. And this is the only pair of pants you will have for 22 days, and you don't get to change them or take a bath. All you get to do is find a stream and maybe take your shoes off and wash your feet and try and splash water on your face and get as clean as you could. But that's all the bathing that you got to do in those 22 days.

FIRST LANDING ON OKINAWA

I remember there was this ray of light that broke through and showed a beautiful sunny day in the making. Of course it would be April 1, Easter Morning of 1945, and probably one that no member of this landing party will ever forget! Many books have been written, and many correspondents have covered this Easter Morning, but it seems that no two are able to describe it in the same way.

Okinawa was the training island for all the artillery in the Japanese army. You can't imagine how many tunnels were in this island and what all was going on underground. Some of the caves stretched from one end of the island to the other. They had worked on it for years and years.

The first amphibious landing on Okinawa was in the northern part of the island and it seemed to go real well; at least I thought it did. Of course, we lost a lot of men in our outfit, but we had secured the northern part of the island.

My lieutenant, Charlie, was with me on Okinawa and we were on patrol. We probably had 25 men on this patrol and we had a man with us who had a dog trained to identify the enemy. As we went down the trail, I was so close to this dog that I said to the man, "Boy, your dog is acting like there's Japanese around." And he said, "Ah, they've been living here for days and days. Look at the fires they've had and the fish heads they've eaten. It still smells like they've been cooking. And I think that's what's disturbing my dog." I said, "Man, I don't know, I have had a lot of dogs in my life and that dog is acting like he's worried and that worries me." Well, about that time we ran into an ambush. They just started shooting all of a sudden and I was on the trail and I think everybody else was on the trail too. Of course everybody tried to jump into the woods, but we lost 13 men in about three seconds.

We could hardly carry the dead and the wounded personnel out that day. We had to get the wounded men to the beach and it was a rough trip. I can remember it was so steep we even had to tie ropes on to the stretcher to keep from tripping and falling down. We were trying to cut through the terrain and get to sickbay as quickly as we could, because we were carrying a badly wounded soldier. It wasn't something that you like to remember, but it's still something that you need to talk about.

After we got there we were just resting; all of us were really tired. Charlie said, "I'm going to have to go to sickbay. I got shot back down on the trail, and it hit me like a ton of bricks. It really was rough." I asked where he was hit. He said, "In the back somewhere. I don't know just where, but it's in my back." I had noticed he kept putting his hand down in his belt and on his back side and then he'd take it out and wipe something on his pants. He didn't want to be obvious and he didn't want to complain, but he said, "I'm going to have to report to sickbay." I tried to talk Charlie out of it by saying "They'll pull you away from here. Let's wait and go back to our unit and then check you in. You'd get to stay in the unit that way." He was sure he needed to report to sickbay, so I said, "Well, let me look at it and let's see what it is. I carry a morphine shot. I can give you a shot." I was kind of kidding and he said, "It's not a joke. It hit me pretty hard." We got to examining him and I couldn't find where the wound was. So I got to looking around and his pack was indeed bloody, but I discovered the shot had gone through a can of tomato puree, and lucky for him that's what was running down his back.

That same day, after taking the wounded to the hospital ship, Charlie and I came upon this big stack of boots there on the beach. Well, we had been wearing the same socks and shoes for 22 days without taking them off. Charlie said, "Pick your size, sit down and put them on." They weren't just clean socks, they were new socks. And they weren't just clean boots, they were new boots. I got mine on and boy, they looked good and felt great. Just as I stood up there was an MP that walked around the corner and he said, "Now just sit down and take them off and place them gently back in the box and put them back where they were." I heard Charlie say, "You ain't got enough bullets in that gun to make me do that." Then he told me to walk away. Charlie was in a Mexican stand-off with this guard and I carefully backed out of there, but Charlie just walked away. I didn't like that situation at all and was scared to death that MP was going to shoot us. But he didn't and we got our new boots and socks.

SECOND LANDING

It was our understanding that after our landing on Okinawa we were headed for a rest, a much needed break and then back to Guadalcanal for more training. But orders came down that we had a 50 mile hike to take. We had to walk from the northern part of the island down to the southern part and then they put us aboard ship. I wondered why they didn't bring the ship up to the northern part of the island and pick us up? It would have been so easy, but there seemed to be something very hush-hush about the whole operation. Well, everybody had a bad case of diarrhea along the trail. When you were so sick you couldn't go any farther, you'd just lay down. Well, the enemy was coming along and slitting the throats of the sick men at night. We had soldiers lying along the trail with their throats cut.

There were a couple wind talkers with us when we made that hike. They were sitting by the trail and one of them was holding his brother who had been shot. He didn't want to leave his brother alone so I stayed behind with them as a guard till the body could be picked up.

Once we got down south they took us out to sea and put us aboard another ship. We had to make another landing on the southern tip of the island.

I was not particularly fond of making my second landing on this island. I spent a great deal of time listening to my ship-to-shore radio, which I would use as a forward observer to fire large guns from our ships. There was a great concern about the thousands of civilians who were now on the southern tip of the island, and the number of casualties expected was skyrocketing. This was where all the personnel, the natives and the people that lived on the island were. All of the Japanese Navy nurses that were stationed in that area had been driven down to the southern part of the island.

When you are a forward observer, you get to be first in everything but the chow line. That day I was awakened at 4:00 a.m. and was told it was time for my team to shimmy down the rope ladder and board a Higgins boat. There would be a short time for a little prayer and to say our thanks for a rather calm ocean. Since I was carrying a 38 pound generator for my team's radio, I was especially thankful for the stillness of the sea.

For several days my lieutenant had been telling me that I might see some black Marines on our next landing. As a kid I was accustomed to being around black people every day — either on the job where I worked or when they would come to our country store to trade.

When I looked to the stern of our landing boat, I saw a black man dressed in Marine uniform that looked so much like Bud Pinkett from Browntown that I almost yelled, "Hi Bud!!" Bud came with his grand-mother, Susie, to my house when she took care of me and my brother. Even though our skin was different in color, I was very fond of Susie and it was a pleasure when she brought Bud along.

While I was reliving days of the past, our Higgins boat had churned its way onto a sandy beach and hit it with a thud. The next sound was a creaking crash as the landing platform made contact with the sand and settled into a comfortable position. I reached down to pick up my gen-erator as a black flash went past me and I wondered how anyone could get from the back of the boat to the front so quickly. I was all set for the race to high ground when I realized my competition was running empty-handed and unarmed into the chaos we'd landed in.

I was wishing I could have had a visit with him when the bullets be-gan to fly and the joys of my youthful years were crowded out by a state of confusion that I have never been able to shake off. The Japanese were running in all directions — civilians, nurses, young men - too young to fill a uniform, and old people unable to get out of the way.

This landing was so strange and different from any landing I had ever known that I didn't seem to be a part of it. I began to wonder if it was only a dream and I would wake up to a beautiful Easter Morning. Then horns began to blow and sirens and bells announced the landing and I grab the heaviest piece of equipment my team had and made the fastest trip I'd ever made toward higher ground.

If you want to know about a nightmare, I can tell you about a night-mare. This was it. Everyone was so bunched together there wasn't a chance for a Marine to operate in the manner that he was trained.

At first those in command wanted to try Naval gunfire. I said, "You can't use it with all these people around. It's not going to work. We're go-ing to end up killing more Marines than we do the enemy. What about getting some explosives men in here?" I was quite surprised when the explosives man arrived. I immediately flashed back to being aboard ship. I can't remember which island it was, but we were on standby and this fellow carried all kinds of supplies in a pack on his back all the time. All he did was sit around and pinch off this material and put it in a wad and play with it. I thought, "Gosh, the man is far out." It was scary to me and I kind of shied away from him. I was Sergeant of the Guard one day and he refused to help. He said, "I don't have time to do it. I got a lot of work to do." And he just sat around tossing those wads up in the air. I didn't realize at the time that he was measuring the weight of the plastic explosives he would be tossing into the enemy's foxholes.

And, that's who showed up, the man who had been tossing the explosive wads, the very man I had almost reported for refusing to do guard duty. He came right up and asked me how I was doing. I was surprised when he spoke to me in such a friendly manner. I could tell that he'd been around on a number of islands before this. When I asked him if he could help us out, he said, "We'll see. What have you got?" And I told him they wanted to try to get all these people out of the caves the Japanese had dug in the hillside. He said, "We'll see what we can do," and walked over and opened that bag and started tossing and catching those wads until he got the size he wanted and then he started throwing them in the holes, running one to the next. I watched as the bodies began flying through the air, arms and legs and human elements of all type, bursting from those caves. And when a body landed beside me, I saw that was a Japanese Navy nurse, dressed in a man's uniform, a woman. It turned out they were all women in these foxholes and caves. And every time he'd throw an explosive in, a couple of them would fly through the air. I had to stop him and told him this is not going to work. He said, "What's the matter? I thought I was doing a pretty good job." I said, "Yeah, but you haven't looked at what you're doing."

We were using plastic explosives followed by 20 or 30 flares to destroy anything left alive. After the assault on one cave I heard something moving and coming forward out of the cave like it was running up a stairway. I figured the enemy was still in there alive and I got ready to shoot when out comes one little Billy Goat and he came straight to me. He was burned all up and scorched all over. How he survived, I do not know. Standing at my feet he reached out and tapped my foot gently and looked up at me.

In a flash of memory, I was in back in Overton; Mom, me, and our Billy Goat are gathered around the heating stove in our dining room. We're doing my homework for school the next day. It was my mother's suggestion that we train Billy to relieve himself in a roasting pan like a kitten in a litter box. Our house had become a place of learning for certain.

One stormy night, as the lightning flashed, the goat ran to my side and tapped gently, but hurriedly, on my bare toe. The sound of thunder was leaving the room when the ping of little black balls hitting the pan took over and then laughter filled the air. "Atta boy, Billy!" but he was gently tapping my bare foot again, as if to say, "Great catch, Fred." I'm pretty certain we were the only people around with a housebroken Billy Goat.

From the first time that little goat ran up to me and tapped on my bare foot with his front hoof, we had a connection and became great friends. Mom said not to be surprised that your pet desires to be friends as much as you do. And now thousands of miles from Overton, one little scorched Billy Goat is tapping my foot. "Atta boy, Billy," and he looked at me and then went on his way.

But we were losing so many men at night that we knew we had to secure those fox holes and caves somehow. We decided to draw straws to see which group would go and clear the caves that night. I came up with the short straw and my forward observer team and I got the job. That night Sy Miller tripped a wire and triggered a land mine. There was a huge explosion and it tore my team of forward observers apart. The top of the cave fell on my legs and arm.

Don't let anyone tell you that you can't remember what happens when you are unconscious, for all of a sudden I could remember the explosion and the Lieutenant from the AGL group saying "I'll take Sy out first. He's in the worst shape." I could also remember him returning and how it hurt so much for him to turn me over and grab the front of my dungaree jacket and start dragging me to the light.

My next remembrance is the screams of an older man. I turned my head so I could see who was there and watched a corpsman take a pair of tweezers and grab burned skin around the neck area and gave a steady pull toward the man's hand. As the mass of skin broke away from his fingertips, I looked to see the face of the person who was lying on the stretcher next to me. It was the oldest man on my forward observer team. He was nearly thirty years old, the father of two children, and husband of a beautiful woman. I had him show me pictures of his family many times and was very sad to witness the news that family would receive.

I was taken to a hospital ship that had been brought in to help with the wounded since we were having so many casualties. I was conscious and awake and also wondering why a ride in a Higgins boat had to be so rough. I began to investigate and realized I had a large tree taped to my right leg and a splint on my right arm. The boat was bouncing so hard that each time it came down I felt I was being beaten to death. The pain was so severe that I passed out again.

When I woke up I was being carried up a floating ramp and onto the deck of a hospital ship. The first thing I saw was a sign that read "Amputation Ward" I began praying that I would not end up there. They took me right on past the door and I said out loud, "Thank you, Lord!" Just as I finished my thank you prayer, they wheeled me right back around and we headed straight through that amputation room door.

SURGEON'S ASSISTANTS

I began to get some feeling back in my right arm and this made me wonder why I was a patient here. Luckily they had not tried to place me on an upper bunk and I was as comfortable as one could be with a tree taped to your side.

Even though I received great attention there seemed to be something that was irritating me – some weird popping sound. I was unable to move my right arm and feel around to see what these little particles were that kept falling on me from the bunk above. I finally asked a corpsman and he said without hesitation, "They're maggots. The doctor wants them left in the boy's leg above you until they can get it amputated. He says they will keep the infection down."

That also explained the sound I kept hearing. The closest description I can come up with is that it's like the first little flakes of a sleet gently hitting the ground and then settling in for a quick melt. And that popping noise is what happens when a maggot wishes to move – he simply plops his tail down on what he is resting on, causing his body to fly off his perch and this is his mode of movement.

As the doctor made his visiting rounds I asked him, "When are you going to do something for me, Doc?" He said, "We take our patients according to what shape they're in. When you get down to where you are the worst one in this ward, then we'll do the amputation." As he walked away I knew I would be feeling sick to my stomach again as the smell of the ward filled my lungs.

THE MAN IN THE MIRROR

When I saw the doctor again I asked if I could take a shower, and he said, "You can do anything that's possible for you to do while you're in this ward." So then I asked, "When can I get this big old tree off my side? All that tape is beginning to make me itch, and I really am not sure that there is a need for it."

"I'll have them take it off" was the only part of his answer I was able to hear as he walked away while taking to me. I totally excused him for this action as I knew he was a very busy person. I hadn't had a shower in many days and when they took the limb off my side, I felt like I could walk a little bit.

I knew my way around a ship, and I went out the door and found the restroom, what we called "the head." There wasn't anybody around when I walked in. There was a long string of stools on one side and a shower stall on the other. I heard the door slam and I looked to see who'd come in. It was somebody I didn't know and I was about to say, "Well, what the hell happened to you?" I looked a little harder and realized I was looking in the mirror. I was looking at myself. I didn't have any hair. It was all burnt off, singed. One eyelid had been cut open and it drooped down and I was looking through the hole in the skin to see out. They hadn't cleaned me up or done anything with me and I was really a ragged looking thing.

It was scary to be in an amputation ward, but the doctor put me to work. He said, "You still got two hands, you ought to be writing the letters for these guys. They can tell you what they want to say to their mothers." So I did and I wrote lots and lots of those letters and it was a hard, hard thing. I did my crying at night. It is difficult to tell or write about, even now.

While I wrote their mothers, I did not write my own because I was unsure what to say. I did not know they had sent my mother a letter saying there had been a huge explosion and they couldn't tell her what had happened but that her son had been "lost in action." They never wrote again or called and I found out later what a hard, hard time my mother had during those 22 days with no word from me.

Eight days and eight nights I spent with that horrible odor and the sound of sawing bones. If I was asked the question, "Where was the worst place you ever served in your tour of duty in the Marines?" my answer would have to be in the amputation ward. The sound of a small saw cutting off an arm or a leg of a young Marine will stay with me for as long as I live.

DAFFODIL THERMOMETER

I'm asked many times if anything funny ever happened during the war and of course it did, even in the amputation ward. A flower arrangement showed up in the ward one day, and the corpsman on duty plucked one of the long-stemmed flowers from the bouquet. He carried his stolen property to the bedside of a Lt. Colonel who had always insisted that the insignias displayed on the collars of clothing he was wearing were very visible. He carried with this the attitude that rank deserved special privileges. This attitude soon began to grow unbearable to the staff of this hospital ship. So with that in mind, the corpsman carrying this beautiful flower said rather loudly, "On your stomach, sir! It's time to take your temperature." He then inserted just enough of the long stem flower to hold it just the way you love to see it sway back and forth in a gentle breeze. He then stepped back to admire his work in the same manner as a great artist would do.

The open door of the amputation ward seemed to gather a crowd of spectators, for no one walking past could continue. No one was laughing, but there were enough chuckles that the colonel turned his head. He saw the crowd that was gathering and said in a practiced voice, "What's wrong with you morons? Haven't you seen a temperature taken rectally before?" There was a sudden stillness in our ward and even the sound of sawing bones was missing, although the smell of sawing bones remained. The quiet of the moment was broken only when one of the swabbies was brave enough to answer the colonel's question, "Yes, sir. I've seen temperatures taken many times rectally, but this is my first time to see it done with a daffodil as a thermometer." When the corpsman was asked where he had gotten that idea, he replied "Reader's Digest."

Another time one of the amputees broke wind so loudly that a corpsman congratulated him and said, "Good one, Charlie!" Charlie yelled back, "You should have heard me when I had two legs!!!" I don't think we ever lost our need for humor.

WAR'S END

I was still in the hospital on Guadalcanal when we dropped the bombs on Hiroshima and Nagasaki. I am glad they dropped them. I think Truman did the right thing and I think those that don't agree with me are wrong. It's that simple. I watched many a man die, you know, and I think he saved many deaths of American soldiers by dropping the bomb. That's just the way I feel. We didn't start it, but we had to end it.

I felt the bombing of Tokyo with the B-25s was also very important, that it was almost equal because that was when things turned around. There's a difference in fighting a war between the early stages when you don't know who is going to win and when you get the upper hand. We got air superiority, we got the army built up and we got a response from the nation. They were making ships and all the things that you need to fight a war.

Thankfully, I managed to keep all my limbs and was dismissed from the hospital ship at Guadalcanal and spent several weeks in a tent as I continued to recover. I happened to be staying right next door to the Red Cross director's tent. I was strolling by one day and thought I'd stop and read the postings on the bulletin board. Down in the corner there was a little note that said, "Oscar Fred Oerly, your father, Henry W. Oerly, has passed away." It was about two weeks old. How easy it would have been for him to walk over and deliver that message to me, but for whatever reason, he didn't.

My father's death wasn't a total surprise to me, because my sister had written and told me that he was very ill and he was going to St. Louis to the Missouri Pacific Hospital. He suspected, I think, that at his age and with his health problems, he may not make it back. At that time, if you were to die in the railroad's hospital, the family could buy a ticket and the railway would take the casket aboard the train and deliver it to the final destination.

When my captain found out about my father's death, he told me he wished he had known about it, because the war was over by then and he could have put me on a plane and sent me home to help my mother bury my dad.

DISCHARGE AND HOME

After being released from the hospital at Guadalcanal we were preparing to occupy Japan. I was helping my group load the ship and my hand was crushed in an accident. It was so bad I lost the fingernails on my left hand and it was terribly painful. I was unable to go with my unit. When they finished loading the ship, they got aboard and left for Japan, and I was headed home. The night before I left, Charlie Pearson handed me a fifth of rum that he had saved for years. The result of that was some very wobbly legs the next morning.

As we were sailing from Guadalcanal to San Diego, where I was to be discharged from the Marines, I was helping the sailors work on their inventory. They were on a zero budget and needed help throwing away all of the food that they weren't going to use before docking their ship in San Diego.

Having spent a lot of time fishing in the Missouri River, it seemed to be great fun to throw a large ham with a great big bone into the ocean and have one of the biggest sharks I had ever seen come to the surface and swallow it in one smooth, graceful move.

My left hand was still very sore, and even though it was painful, when I saw another big shark swimming toward us I grabbed a crate full of oranges and threw it overboard. It was also a thrill to see the grace of that shark as he seemed to make a slight roll to one side. When the crate hit the water the shark took it all in one big gulp.

I knew the shark would never hear me when I yelled, "I hope that gives you one hell of a gut ache!" My sailor friend who was helping me said, "It won't bother him! In two days time a shark has enough acid in his system to dissolve any amount of nails, steel or wire he can swallow."

A few days after I was discharged and examined, I was given the money for the purchase of a ticket on the railway that would transport me from San Diego back to Kansas City. Before going home I wanted to stop in Los Angeles and visit my sister, Marie. She now had a young boy who was old enough for me to push up and down the street, and I did this with pride, telling all who asked about the baby, "He is my nephew! Isn't he great?"

I took the train from San Diego back home. As I listened to the rumbling and squeaking of the troop train, going at top speed, it was easy to tell that the rails of this cross-country railroad had served well in the last four years in transporting men and equipment to all points on its designated route.

It was great to be a civilian again, and I tried to forget the many dangers that followed each and every man enlisted in the Marine Corps. It felt so good to sit and relax knowing that my girlfriend Jan would be at Union Station with a group of friends to celebrate my homecoming in Missouri. I was thankful that I had slept so much on this trip and I felt great. I was enjoying the memories of home and I hoped somehow things hadn't changed in the 38 months since I'd left home.

It was a good thing I had slept so much on the train, because Jan and I, her sister Jean, and Jean's friend, talked all night. This seemed to be an indication of how happy I was to be home.

By the time my unit made it back to the states, Jan and I were married and living in Los Angeles. They had spent several months in Japan with the occupational force and I would have been with them but my hand was so slow to heal and they ended up having to remove my fingernails.

Both Jan and I had found work in LA and we were expecting our first child. I got a phone call and it was one of my group who said, "We're coming though LA and that's where we're splitting up and going our separate ways. Is there a way that we could get to see you?" I took off work and picked Jan up from the store where she was working and we went to see them. If I remember right, Bob Webber was in the group, Don Goodwin, and Max Love. I cannot recall all of them, but there were six that stopped and waited until I got there and we visited with them for awhile.

Purple Hearts are given when a soldier is wounded or killed. I should have had quite a few. It didn't mean that much to me, but it became very important to my new wife, Jan. She wrote President Truman listing all my injuries. He eventually answered her, and the letter said they had record of one injury that they can issue a Purple Heart for. That was the only one I received. She felt I deserved a Purple Heart for every one of my wounds but after writing many letters, she finally let it go.

WHAT REMAINS?

I was discharged with a report that I had 38 pieces of shrapnel still in my body, one piece for every month I had served. Shrapnel is what we call the fragments of high-explosive shells that tear into your body. Some of it I had cut out and paid for with my own insurance. I was not treated well by the Veteran's Administration, and that lifelong health care President Roosevelt promised me never materialized. I had four pieces removed by Dr. Alex Van Ravenswaay in his clinic here in Boonville after I started working as a bricklayer. I remember one day I scratched my back where I had this bump that was itching and my finger felt funny. I looked and it was just bleeding to beat the band. I had a piece of shrapnel sticking through my skin and it had cut the end of my finger. I went to see Dr. Alex and he took it out.

Another time I had a big knot come up under my jaw and I went back to have him work on that one too. He spoke with a thick accent and I can remember him picking up his operating knife and saying, "Now vhistle." After he said it for the third time, I said, "Dr. Alex, why do you keep asking me to whistle when you're cuttin' on my jaw?" He said, "Vell, vhat vay I can tell if I'm cutting a nerve or not." Man, at that moment I wished I had told my wife I was having that operation. He had me whistling all the while he's cutting out a piece of shrapnel the size of my thumb, and it was mighty close to my throat.

The doctor would then send the shrapnel to the hospital so they could record the removal and keep track of how many pieces I had left in me. When they list you with 38 pieces, you got a few more to look for. You can find one just about any time you want to. I got one that came up the other day. It makes a bump and then a growth around it and I'll have to have that cut out, too. Shrapnel moves around and that's the danger because it can affect a vital organ and you're just lucky if it makes its way out and doesn't cause you trouble. They should have taken a lot more out than they did. I don't even know how much is left in my body. There are a whole lot of veterans walking around with shrapnel in them, and they will be until the day they die.

Like I said, I don't dwell on the war all the time; I carve things out of wood. I carved and painted 112 cardinals for the volunteers who take the veterans here in Missouri on the Honor Flights up to see the memorials in Washington D.C. That's a lot of cardinals. Now I'm working on hummingbirds, and of course, I've carved my share of bears.

ONLINE ACCESS,
DOCUMENTS & PHOTOS

ONLINE ACCESS to 38 _Pieces of Shrapnel_

This book and related audio recordings and files can be found online in the University of Missouri's digital archive, MOspace. To find my collection, go to http://mospace.umsystem.edu and search for Fred Oerly, or visit this permanent web link: http://hdl.handle.net/10355/43596.

1. Interview of Fred, conducted by his grandson, for U S Congressional Library's Veterans History Project
2. The transcript of that interview. This transcript along with Fred's hand written notes were the sources for this book.
3. An audio reading of this book "38 pieces of Shrapnel" read by Fred's grandson, Mitch Hughey.
4. A PDF version of this book to enable ease of searching through changes in media and formats.
5. Typed version of Fred's handwritten notes describing his war experiences.
    NOTE: for best performance, download the audio files and then play them from your local computer or other digital playback device.

ADDITIONAL WEB SITES FOR MORE INFORMATION

An enormous amount of information has been released by the US government including many photos and videos. One need simply search for a wealth of internet content. Here are some recommended sites:

Wikipedia (the free encyclopedia) has a wealth of relevant information including:
   http://en.wikipedia.org/wiki/Bougainville_Campaign
   http://en.wikipedia.org/wiki/Battle_of_Saipan
   http://en.wikipedia.org/wiki/Battle_of_okinawa
   http://en.wikipedia.org/wiki/Battle_of_Guam_(1944)
   http://en.wikipedia.org/wiki/Code_talker
   http://en.wikipedia.org/wiki/6th_Marine_Division_(United_States)
   http://en.wikipedia.org/wiki/Pacific_Ocean_theater_of_World_War_II
   http://en.wikipedia.org/wiki/Pacific_War

Navy Historical Center's Guadalcanal Campaign, August 1942 - February 1943
   Includes a variety of photos.
   http://www.history.navy.mil/photos/events/wwii-pac/guadlcnl/guadlcnl.htm

National Public Radio & National Geographic Society's Radio Expeditions – Sixty years after The Battle for Guadalcanal
   http://www.npr.org/templates/story/story.php?storyId=1147881

Navy Seabees on Guadalcanal
   http://www.seabeecook.com/history/canal/cactus.htm

Official web site of the Third Marine Division
   http://www.3rdmardiv.marines.mil

Official Web Site of the Sixth Marine Division
   http://www.sixthmarinedivision.com
   See info on Battle of Okinawa at:
   http://www.sixthmarinedivision.com/Battle%20of%20Okinawa.html

Battle of Okinawa Statistics
http://www.jahitchcock.com/okibattle.html

The Invasion of Saipan – documents the strategic importance of Saipan, the Japanese defense of the island, and the United States invasion of the island of Saipan.
https://sites.google.com/site/blodgetthistoricalconsulting/the-invasion-of-saipan

Radio News account of Victory in Japan Day
http://www.otr.com/vj.html

Navajo Code Talkers
http://www.msnbc.com/the-last-word/last-wwii-navajo-code-talkers-dies

http://indiancountrytodaymedianetwork.com/2013/12/19/navajo-code-talker-wilfred-e-billey-walks-152748

http://www.history.navy.mil/faqs/faq61-2.htm http://history1900s.about.com/od/worldwarii/a/navajacode.htm

MAPS

Interactive map depicting World War II in the Pacific
http://www.eduplace.com/kids/socsci/books/applications/imaps/maps/g5s_u8

World War II Battles - Pacific Theater 1941-1945 – This map plots the locations of and chronologically orders the 131 significant World War II battles and campaigns in the Pacific theater from 1941-1945.
https://maps.google.com/maps/ms?ie=UTF8&oe=UTF8&msa=0&msid=211710981847614598414.0004750e252ca4e35f3c0&dg=feature

YouTube VIDEOS

A&E's Lost Evidence series of videos including:
Guadalcanal: http://www.youtube.com/watch?v=FqO32Lpgq5E
Guam: http://www.youtube.com/watch?v=K5Jk0QUowNM
Saipan: http://www.youtube.com/watch?v=zNusk-NUoWs
Okinawa: http://www.youtube.com/watch?v=Ql1alwZcvck

From the series of "Rare Color Film World War II"
Aircraft Carriers in the Pacific: http://www.youtube.com/watch?v=9dR3h2HdnBQ
Guadalcanal: http://www.youtube.com/watch?v=2KZhddZcfqM
Saipan: https://www.youtube.com/watch?v=YIgpluBCzpI&feature=related
Okinawa, Japan's Last Stand: https://www.youtube.com/watch?v=CtN1e7Rdt2Y

Sixth Marine Division on Okinawa (50 minutes)
http://www.youtube.com/watch?v=gF9-LA2nQBo

Saipan and Tinian
http://navysite.de/ships/lha2about.htm

http://militaryhistory.about.com/od/worldwarii/p/World-War-Ii-Battle-Of-Saipan.htm

Marine Corps black and white video re Tinian: http://www.youtube.com/watch?v=UGWK4K2xFkM

45 Minute recreated documentary on the battle of Guadalcanal (you are in the cockpit) http://www.youtube.com/watch?v=hUsOQyfnfDY

DEPARTMENT OF THE NAVY
HEADQUARTERS UNITED STATES MARINE CORPS
WASHINGTON 25. D. C.

IN REPLY REFER TO
DLA-geg
426722
2 6 JAN 1959

Mr. O. Fred Oerly
908 Kemper Drive
Boonville, Missouri

My dear Mr. Oerly:

The records of this Headquarters show that you are entitled to the following awards for your services while a member of the U. S. Marine Corps.

Bronze Star Medal with Combat "V"	1 Apr to 7 Jun 1945	Okinawa, Ryukyu Islands
Purple Heart	7 Jun 1945	Okinawa, Ryukyu Islands
Asiatic-Pacific Campaign Medal with 3 bronze stars	1943-1945	Treasury-Bougainville; Marianas Operation; Okinawa
Victory Medal	1942-1945	World War II

The Bronze Star Medal and Purple Heart are being forwarded to you this date under separate cover by certified mail. The records show that the temporary citation for the Bronze Star Medal was presented to you in the field and the permanent citation was forwarded to you on 6 October 1948.

There are enclosed a certificate for the Purple Heart, the Asiatic-Pacific Campaign Medal and Victory Medal, World War II.

Stars and ribbon bars for campaign and service medals are not issued by this Headquarters; however, they may be purchased from most local military shops or either of the following firms:

N. S. Meyer, Inc.　　　　　　A. H. Dondero, Inc.
419 Fourth Avenue　　　　　1718 Pennsylvania Avenue, N. W.
New York 16, New York　　Washington, D. C.

Sincerely yours,

upwhite

V. P. WHITE
Head, Decorations and Medals Branch
By direction of the Commandant of the Marine Corps

Encl:
(1) (SC) Bronze Star Medal and Purple Heart
(2) Purple Heart Certificate
(3) Asiatic-Pacific Campaign Medal and
　　Victory Medal, World War II

The President of the United States takes pleasure in presenting the BRONZE STAR MEDAL to

SERGEANT FRED O. OERLY,
UNITED STATES MARINE CORPS RESERVE,

for service as set forth in the following

CITATION:

"For meritorious achievement as Team Chief of the Sixth Joint Assault Signal Company, Headquarters Battalion, Sixth Marine Division, during operations against enemy Japanese forces on Okinawa, Ryukyu Islands, from 1 April to 7 June 1945. Efficiently directing his team, Sergeant Oerly established and maintained effective communications, thereby contributing to the success of his Battalion. His skillful leadership, courage and devotion to duty were in keeping with the highest traditions of the United States Naval Service."

Sergeant Oerly is authorized to wear the Combat "V"

For the President,

Secretary of the Navy.

IN REPLYING ADDRESS
COMMANDANT OF THE MARINE CORPS
WASHINGTON 25, D. C.
AND REFER TO

SERIAL 426722
DGP-298-vlb

for PEACE
OF
MIND—
BUY
SAVINGS
BONDS

HEADQUARTERS U. S. MARINE CORPS
WASHINGTON

OCT 6 – 1948

My dear Mr. Oerly:

    I take pleasure in forwarding to you the enclosed permanent citation for the Bronze Star Medal previously presented you in the name of the President of the United States for meritorious achievement during operations against enemy Japanese forces on Okinawa, Ryukyu Islands, from 1 April to 7 June 1945, with the United States Marine Corps.

    Be assured of my deep appreciation of your devotion to duty and gallant action which were in keeping with the highest traditions of the United States Marine Corps.

        Sincerely yours,

        C. B. CATES
        General, U.S.M.C.
        Commandant of the Marine Corps

Enclosure: 1.

Mr. Fred O. Oerly,
    1350 West 47th Street,
        Los Angeles, California.

FOR VICTORY
BUY
UNITED
STATES
WAR
BONDS
AND
STAMPS

SERIAL 426722
DGU-893-ch

HEADQUARTERS U. S. MARINE CORPS
WASHINGTON

29 June, 1945.

My dear Mr. and Mrs. Oerly:

    A brief report has just been received that your son, Sergeant Oscar F. Oerly, USMCR, sustained a blast concussion in action against the enemy on 7 June, 1945 at Okinawa Island, Ryukyu Islands.

    Your anxiety is realized, and you may be sure that any additional details or information received will be forwarded to you at the earliest possible moment. Please notify this office of any change in your address.

Sincerely yours,

JOSEPHUS DANIELS, JR.,
Captain, U. S. Marine Corps.

Mr. and Mrs. Henry W. Oerly,
   P. O. Box #24,
     Overton, Missouri.

THE UNITED STATES OF AMERICA

TO ALL WHO SHALL SEE THESE PRESENTS, GREETING:

THIS IS TO CERTIFY THAT

THE PRESIDENT OF THE UNITED STATES OF AMERICA
HAS AWARDED THE

PURPLE HEART

ESTABLISHED BY GENERAL GEORGE WASHINGTON
AT NEWBURGH, NEW YORK, AUGUST 7, 1782

TO

Fred G. Gerly

FOR WOUNDS RECEIVED
IN ACTION

June 7, 1945, while Sergeant, U.S. Marine Corps Reserve

GIVEN UNDER MY HAND IN THE CITY OF WASHINGTON
THIS   26th   DAY OF   January   1959

P. M. Pate

GENERAL, U.S. MARINE CORPS
COMMANDANT OF THE MARINE CORPS

Fred Oerly, after basic training

Fred and Sam Oerly

Guadalcanal - Sam Oerly, back row, third from right

Islanders on Guadalcanal

Bougainville 1945

On guard

Marines at base camp, Guadalcanal

Guadalcanal 1944, taken by Fred Oerly

Guadalcanal base camp

Shower at base camp, Guadalcanal

Guadalcanal urinal

6th Marine Joint Assault Signal Corps Headquarters

Fred Oerly, on right

Fred Oerly, home from the war.

Fred and Jan Oerly, engaged at Thanksgiving,
married at Christmas, 1945.

SAMUEL HENRY OERLY (SILENT$^\lambda$ SAM), Major, USMC, born Oct. 7, 1920, Overton, MO.

Enlisted March 3, 1941, boot training: Camp Pendleton, CA. Fought in the Pacific in WW II with the 3rd Marine Division: Bougainville, Guadalcanal and Guam. Completed flight training Oct. 6, 1946 at Pensacola.

Completed aviation electronics course; taught electronics for 3 1/2 years in addition to his pilot duties. Flew 150 combat missions in Korea; promoted to second lieutenant on Oct. 3, 1952.

Taught leadership school at El Toro for a year, then sent to Pensacola as a flight instructor. Completed helicopter training at Ellyson Field.

Other assignments include: Helicopter Transport Squadron 461, at New River, NC; flight deck officer aboard USS *Boxer;* Cherry Point, NC; Seattle Marine Reserve Detachment; others.

He helped put the light house dome at Cape Fear, NC; first Marine officer to be flight deck officer on a Navy carrier.

His medals/awards include: Rifle Expert, Pistol Expert, Distinguished Flying Cross, six Air Medals, Good Conduct, Armed Forces, Korean Service and the National Defense.

Spent over 26 years in the Corps before being killed on active duty June 29, 1966. Married to Anne and they had two daughters.